❀ SUFI WISDOM SERIES

SYMPHONY OF REMEMBRANCE

BY
SHAYKH MUHAMMAD HISHAM KABBANI

Foreword
by
Shaykh Muhammad Nazim Adil Al-Haqqani
World Leader of the Most Distinguished
Naqshbandi Sufi Order

February 2003 -June 2003
Indonesia, Detroit, Oakland, Palo Alto.

INSTITUTE FOR SPIRITUAL AND CULTURAL
ADVANCEMENT

© Copyright 2007 by the **Institute for Spiritual and Cultural Advancement.** All rights reserved.
ISBN: 1-930409-49-4
No part of this book may be reproduced, stored in a retrieval system, or transmitted in any form, or by any means, electronic, mechanical, photocopying, or otherwise, without the written permission of the **Institute for Spiritual and Cultural Advancement.**

Library of Congress Cataloging-in-Publication Data

TBD

Published and Distributed by:
Institute for Spiritual and Cultural Advancement
17195 Silver Parkway, #201 Fenton, MI 48430 USA
Tel: (888) 278-6624
Fax:(810) 815-0518
Email: staff@islamicsupremecouncil.org
Web: http://www.islamicsupremecouncil.org

Shaykh Muhammad Nazim Adil al-Haqqani (right), world leader of the most distinguished Naqshbandi-Haqqani Sufi Order, with his representative, and author of this book, Shaykh Muhammad Hisham Kabbani.

The seven heavens and the earth, and all beings therein, declare His glory: there is not a thing but celebrates His praise; And yet ye understand not how they declare His glory!

Holy Qur'an: Isra (The Night Journey), 17:44

TABLE OF CONTENTS

Editor's Notes ix
About the Author xiii
Preface 15
Numerology of 'Ya' and 'Sin' 21
Watch After Your Trust 31
The Preciousness of the Prophet's Blood 39
Wars of the Last Days 49
Getting Good Grades for Your Afterlife 63
The Symphony of Remembrance in the Era of Shah Naqshband 79
Stop Laughing, Begin to Cry 89
Guide Your Flock to the Right Way 95
Raise Your Children in Innocence 103
Where is Moses? 119
Young People Raised in Islam 129
Seven Dates 143
The Importance of Marriage 145
Are You Building an Ark Like Noah? 153
Muslims of the West are the Examples for the Muslims of the East 159
Heavenly Technology: Source of Earthly Technology 165
Do Not Delay Marriage and Make It Difficult! 173
Glossary 181

EDITOR'S NOTES

This book consists of the teachings of Mawlana Shaykh Hisham Kabbani ق, the authorized representative in the West of Mawlana Shaykh Nazim al-Qubrusi ق. Mawlana Shaykh Nazim ق is the Sultan of Saints, the Grandshaykh of the Most Distinguished Naqshbandi Sufi Way, he holds the attention and love of millions of followers around the world. Our only hope is that they both be pleased with this work.

These are associations and Friday Prayer sermons given mainly in California in the late winter and spring of 2003. We present them largely in the same format in which they were given in order to preserve the spirit and charm of their transmission to all humanity. Wherever we could, we gave the date and place of each association (*suhba*).

As this book was designed to be accessible to non-Muslims, we have taken out many Arabic words and the original Arabic Qur'anic and hadith (traditions of the Holy Prophet Muhammad ﷺ) language, leaving only the English translation. Some limited use of Arabic words remains—for instance "Sayyidina" for "Our master." Where Arabic words are important to and explained by the substance of the text, they have, by and large, been left out.

Since the original material was an oral transmission, extensive liberties were taken with the structure of the talks: there are some revisions of language that make it more readable in written form, talks on the same subject were compiled, and the addition of scientific and religious references were added where necessary. However, we have tried our best to retain the full flavor and essence of Shaykh Hisham's talks. We take full responsibility for these changes, and ask our shaykh's and our reader's forgiveness for any errors in the final text.

Citations from the Qur'an are footnoted with the chapter (*surah*) and verse number (e.g. 25:20) for easy look-up. The Traditions of the Holy Prophet ﷺ which have been placed in the text are without full chains of transmission, but are firmly established hadith and should be familiar to and immediately accepted on sight by the vast majority of Muslims and certainly scholars.

For people knowledgeable about Arabic and Islam: we apologize for the vastly simplified transliteration style used in the body of this. Our experience has been that transliteration symbols, when unfamiliar, make for heavy and difficult reading. Since this book is designed to be inviting and accessible to people without extensive knowledge of Arabic or Islam, we have omitted most diacritic marks with the notable exception of the letter '*ayn*' represented by '''. We ask for your patience with this compromise between accuracy and accessibility.

We use the personal pronouns "he" and "him" when speaking about a person who may be male or female—"he" is less awkward than the other solutions to this problem. We do not wish to offend women who read the book; this decision is only to improve flow of the text.

The following symbols are universally recognized by Muslims and have been respectfully included in this work:

> The symbol ﷻ represents *subhaanahu wa ta'ala*, (may His Glory be Exalted) praise customarily recited after reading or pronouncing the name "Allah" and any of the Islamic names of God.

Editor's Notes

The symbol ﷺ represents *sall-Allahu 'alayhi wa sallam* (God's blessings and greetings of peace be upon him), which is customarily recited after reading or pronouncing the holy name of Prophet Muhammad.

The symbol ﷺ represents *'alayhis-salam* (peace be upon him/her), which is customarily recited after reading or pronouncing the holy names of the other prophets, family members of Prophet Muhammad, the pure and virtuous women in Islam, and the angels.

The symbol ؓ represents *radi-Allahu 'anh* (may God be pleased with him/her), which is customarily recited after reading or pronouncing the holy names of companions of the Prophet ﷺ.

The symbol ق represents *qaddas-Allahu sirrah* (may God sanctify his secret), which is customarily recited after reading or pronouncing the name of a saint.

ABOUT THE AUTHOR

Shaykh Muhammad Hisham Kabbani is a world-renowned author and religious scholar. He has devoted his life to the promotion of the traditional Islamic principles of peace, tolerance, love, compassion and brotherhood, while opposing extremism in all its forms. The shaykh is a member of a respected family of traditional Islamic scholars, which includes the former head of the Association of Muslim Scholars of Lebanon and the present Grand Mufti[1] of Lebanon.

In the U.S., Shaykh Kabbani serves as Chairman, Islamic Supreme Council of America; Founder, Naqshbandi Sufi Order of America; Advisor, World Organization for Resource Development and Education; Chairman, As-Sunnah Foundation of America; Chairman, Kamilat Muslim Women's Organization; and, Founder and President, The Muslim Magazine.

Shaykh Kabbani is highly trained, both as a Western scientist and as a classical Islamic scholar. He received a bachelor's degree in chemistry and studied medicine. In addition, he also holds a degree in Islamic Divine Law, and under the tutelage of Shaykh 'Abd Allah Daghestani ق, license to teach, guide and counsel religious students in Islamic spirituality from Shaykh Muhammad Nazim 'Adil al-Qubrusi al-Haqqani an-Naqshbandi ق, the world leader of the Naqshbandi-Haqqani Sufi Order.

---

[1] The highest Islamic religious authority in the country.

His books include: *A Spiritual Commentary on the Chapter of Sincerity* (2006), *Sufi Science of Self-Realization* (Fons Vitae, 2005), *Keys to the Divine Kingdom* (2005); *Classical Islam and the Naqshbandi Sufi Order* (2004); *The Naqshbandi Sufi Tradition Guidebook* (2004); *The Approach of Armageddon? An Islamic Perspective* (2003); *Encyclopedia of Muhammad's Women Companions and the Traditions They Related* (1998, with Dr. Laleh Bakhtiar); *Encyclopedia of Islamic Doctrine* (7 vols. 1998); *Angels Unveiled* (1996); *The Naqshbandi Sufi Way* (1995); *Remembrance of God Liturgy of the Sufi Naqshbandi Masters* (1994).

In his long-standing endeavor to promote better understanding of classical Islam, Shaykh Kabbani has hosted two international conferences in the United States, both of which drew scholars from throughout the Muslim world. As a resounding voice for traditional Islam, his counsel is sought by journalists, academics and government leaders.

Preface

The Whole Universe is an Orchestra of Divine Glorification

Glorifying Allah is what gives real life. Nothing can be sweeter for our souls than to make *dhikrullah,* our Lord's remembrance! Angels lives come from their *tasbeeh,* glorification, saying: "*Subhanallah, Sultan-Allah*—Glory be—to God, God is King!"

There are countless kinds and forms of glorification. Everything is glorifying Allah; everything! Everything has a private structure and personality. We cannot find throughout creation, even through multiple universes, anything to be on the same characteristics as any other creation. Each has its distinct unique personality.

You may take atoms—for example hydrogen is an element and it is different from oxygen. Further, do you think that every atom of hydrogen is the same? If they are the same, they must combine, but every atom is keeping its personality, never are two atoms coming together, no. It is the same for atoms, for each atom has its private personality, so that one hydrogen atom is not becoming combined with the next hydrogen atom. If it were to be joined with another hydrogen, it will have only a single nucleus and around it orbiting two electrons. In that case it is another creation—it is no longer hydrogen. Therefore each one is keeping its personality.

Every atom is holding its private, special personality, just as you are not going to be similar to your son or daughter but different Therefore while there are billions of human beings they are all separate and each one has a special personality. You are special, having a specialty that making you different from the next person, from the third person and in fact from all others.

And also, each individual atom has a name—a private name—that was granted to that atom from its Lord, its Creator. It is also given a different kind of glorification so that one atom's glorifying is different from the next one's. Each one has a different glorification, so that every one is glorifying in a different manner and thus the glorification of atoms cannot be counted.

You may look at an orchestra. A symphony may be composed of twenty different kinds of instruments: Flutes, drums, horns, violins, trombones, even a piano, how many! Each one is glorifying its Lord with a different form of glorification. We say: "*Subhanallah, Sultan-Allah!*" This is glorifying. But at the same time everything from which our structure has been created, each atom and each part is glorifying and praising God by itself and altogether they are making a kind of orchestra—their glorifying coming in such a way that if you could hear it you would fall down in a faint!

Glorifying Allah Almighty is what Allah Almighty granted to His creatures: to praise and magnify their Lord and the whole universe is such a symphony of perfect glorification! "Allah, Allah, Allah Allah!" Yes, we ask Allah Almighty to grant us His endless Blessings to hear the glorification of all things.

The most beautiful glorifying comes from water! Waters' glorification of God is so majestic that it is giving life to the dead, making them to come to life. Water is bringing everything from death to life. Without water, nothing is coming to life. Therefore the secret, *sirr*, Allah Almighty granted only to water, is majestic, because that is bringing life to the dead: "Allah Allah!"

Preface

We made from water every living thing[2]

For every creation there must be a master power from water in order to come into existence, to be alive. Earthly water is all the same. "Do you know how many kinds of water?" "Yes, Sir, we know: spring water, rain water, ocean water..." so many different kinds!

That is what you know! In reality you cannot count the kinds of water! All things, from being nothing, He is bringing to be something and causing to come alive through the secret power that Allah Almighty has granted to water. That power is required for life. And there are so many kinds of water, but those you know are only rain water, river water, well water, ocean water. They are the same, but in reality there are so many kinds of water that bring life to created beings. They were nothing and then they are coming to be something!

Therefore, according to the traditional knowledge of the Prophet that is reaching to saints[3] and the Companions[4] from the Prophet ﷺ, they were reaching to such a level that they were able to hear the *"tasbeehu 'l-miyah"*—the glorification of water! When a person finally reaches to such a level that his physical being can no longer support it, there will appear at that time another personality. From that different water, Allah is bringing people from one level, the lowest level, to the highest, and their glorifying is going to be much much more—endless without stopping! Therefore—angels are making glorification and from that are living!

---

[2] Suratu 'l-Anbiya (The Prophets), 21:30.
[3] Arabic: *Awliya*.
[4] Arabic: *Sahaba*.

O people, if you are asking real life, happy life, peaceful life, you must continue to make *tasbeeh*, to glorify your Lord, Almighty Allah! Then you are reaching to a level that you are not in need to eat or to drink, because in that level eating and drinking is completely different. Such a person will never be ill; no need to take anything for a cure, water is enough!

Therefore people bring water to me and say, "O Shaykh, blow on this water!" That is another *sirr*, secret power. People may say: "What is the shaykh doing? Blowing on water and giving it to people?" I am saying: "You are ignorant; you have no understanding of such things so don't ask! Your level, like donkeys or sheep, is to eat straw and grass; go there, it is for you! Don't say: 'We are not understanding,' because it is not your level! You cannot understand!"

Therefore, O people, we are doing *tasbeeh*, glorifying God Almighty and that is what gives you real life, at least you can smell the higher levels refreshment and beauty and endless possibilities are opening to you through that level! Keep on glorifying!

Therefore we are making *tasbeeh* after every prayer. If you can keep that glorification and continue to make *tasbeeh*, then you will reach a level at which you are no longer in need to drink or eat from the level of animals. Now we are drinking and eating at the level of animals, but there is a level far above which gives far more pleasure; much more love; much more peace; much more happiness; much more wisdom; much more power; much more divine Beauty Oceans!

There is a saying that Aphrodite was coming out of the sea at the island of Paphos, and that she was the symbol of Divine Beauty. On that level, when you are reaching the Oceans of Beauty, your mind will leave you! *Tasbeeh* is what carries people to reach there; to happiness oceans, peace oceans, wisdom oceans, knowledge oceans, but people are insisting: "No, we are asking only what is here, at whatever we are able to look and see."

O people, therefore, try to make much more *tasbeeh*, to say: "*Subhanallah, Alhamdulillah, Allahu akbar*"...After daily prayers every time we are repeating these phrases 33 times. Those keeping the level of spirituality in Islam, *tariqah*, repeat at least 100 times a day "Glory be to God, Praise be to God and God is the most great!" Every *tasbeeh* is taking you up from the level of animals to the real level of mankind who are the caliphs, deputies, of Allah Almighty. Whoever is living on this level, the level of animals, will never be deputies, it is impossible.

Allah said to the Prophet Dawud ﷺ, King David, "We have made you a divine representative on earth and we are granting every demand you wish."[5] When someone is reaching that level, finishing, then you are reaching to be as Prophet David ﷺ, where God Almighty was addressing to him: "We are making you now, when you are leaving every kind of selfish desire that belongs to your physical being, when you are leaving it and glorifying your Lord, we are making you a divine deputy on earth..."

Which earth? It is a special earth for you alone without partner! You are reaching to a universe that it is belongs to you alone! O people, we know nothing while Allah knows everything!

Therefore, the most distinguished Naqshbandi Order is taking people and carrying them from their animal being to the level of angels' being. When you are reaching to that level that only angels are there—there are no animals there—you can find your real being there, at that time they put on your head the crown of Divine servanthood—being a devout servant to Allah Almighty.

---

[5] C.f. Surah Saba (Sheba), 34:10,11.

That is granted to you and also a special, blessed dressing that it is the sign of glorifying God Almighty. You have achieved that level.

O people, every kind of praying that God Almighty ordered to His most beloved servant to make is to raise you from the level of animals to the level of Heavenly Existenct, Malakut.

May God forgive us and grant us from the secret knowledge and the secret powers of glorification! May He make us to run after it and to reach to the level of angels in this world.

May Allah Almighty forgive us and lead us and send us some people that are guiding mankind to those levels. If not, we are all on the level of animals!

This book, by Shaykh Hisham Effendi, my son-in-law, is giving information from those levels, and may be so helpful for those people who are asking to reach above the level of animal character.

May Allah forgive me and bless you for the honor of the most honored Prophet and servant in His Divine Presence, Sayyidina Muhammad ﷺ. Al-Fatiha!

Shaykh Muhammad Nazim Adil al-Haqqani
Lefke, Cyprus
April 22, 2007

Numerology of 'Ya' and 'Sin'

[The shaykh addressed a gathering celebrating the completion of memorization of the Holy Qur'an by a young man.]

The Prophet said, "There are two phrases, light on the tongue but heavy in the Balance. They are: "Glory to God and praise Him, Glory to God the Great; may God forgive me." The Imam who spoke before me has already said every possible thing in regard to love of the Prophet ﷺ, and I feel shy to speak after him. I have nothing to add. But since he insisted, I will say something.

It is a tremendous blessing to raise your child studying and memorizing the Holy Qur'an.

The Prophet ﷺ predicted our current situation 1,400 years ago. How did he know, if God did not give him this knowledge?

I did not understand what the previous speaker said in Urdu. But I immediately thought of the meaning of the verse:

> We did indeed offer the trust to the Heavens and the Earth and the mountains; but they refused to undertake it, being afraid thereof: but man undertook it;- He was indeed unjust and foolish; [7]

---

[6] Arabic: *subhanallah wa bi-hamdihi subhanallah il-'adheem istaghfirullah.* This expression, when recited in a group, is one of the most beautiful parts of the Naqshbandi liturgy for the pre-dawn prayer.

[7] Suratu 'l-Ahzab (The Confederates), 33:72.

God asked the heavens, earth, skies and mountains to carry the trust. They said, "No." The mountains were afraid to carry the trust because they would shatter to dust under its weight.

Who carried the trust? Who had that power? Sayyidina Muhammad ﷺ. That means he was able to carry the Qur'an in his heart without being destroyed and shattered.

Sayyida 'Ayesha ؇ said, "The Prophet's character was the Qur'an." We hope that one day we will be able to follow in his footsteps and carry that dress of piety and sincerity and beauty of the Holy Qur'an.

First and Last

As I was looking at that frame on the wall and I saw that it is written there: *YaSeen*[8]

Seeing this verse brought to my mind an explanation. If we look very deeply into this verse, you can see the greatness that God has given to Prophet ﷺ. The two letters *Ya* and *Seen* are, when together, one of the names of Prophet ﷺ.

The Holy Qur'an is the Ancient Words of God, and it is recited in Arabic. The Arabic alphabet is generally considered to consist of 28 letters. In reality it is 29 letters when you include the special combined letters *Lam-alif* as a separate character. So the *lam* and the *alif* together makes another letter. So the alphabet consists of either 28 or 29 letters.

And if you look at the lunar calendar month of the *Hijri* year, it is usually 29 days. If you look at the astrological chart, it

---

[8] Surah YaSeen, 36:1. YaSeen ﷺ is also one of the names of Prophet ﷺ, and is the name of the chapter of which it is the first verse.

consists of 29 different houses. So you see all of these things are based on the number 29.

Also, it is said in the biographies of the Prophet ﷺ that he represents the 29 mansions of the stars, because he is accompanying this whole universe. This is because God created the Prophet ﷺ before creating anything else, and in fact created everything else from him. This was shown by the one hadith, "I was a Prophet when Adam was between clay and water."

The First Creation

Another relevant hadith is, "O Jabir, the first thing God created was the light of your Prophet ﷺ from His light..." The first thing created was light. The light is an indication, through scientific theory, showing that an explosion makes light.

Today's scientists say that when this universe was created there was an explosion, the Big Bang. So that great light from which God created the universe was from the light of Muhammad ﷺ. He was accompanying all of creation because he is the representative of creation.

God said that the phrase *"La ilaha ill-Allah, Muhammadun Rasulullah,* so *Muhammadun Rasulullah*—there is no god except Allah and Muhammad is the Prophet of Allah," represents the creation in the Divine Presence. So immediately the Prophet's name and creation followed *La ilaha ill-Allah*. The fact of Prophet's ﷺ name literally following God's Name in the testimony of faith shows that he follows the Creator. The creation cannot be separated from the Creator in worship. The Creator can be separated from the creation, but the creation cannot be separated from the Creator, it is dependent. The Creator is independent of creation. That is why *La ilaha illa-Allah*, can stand by itself.

But then God is the Creator of whom? He created all created beings to tell them, "You are my servants and I am your Creator."

Who is mentioned in Qur'an as "God's servant"? The Prophet ﷺ is the only one mentioned as servant to the Creator. So the only one who truly represents creation is the Prophet ﷺ—he represents the creation in the Presence of God.

Prophet ﷺ said, "I am the master of the sons of Adam and I say it without pride." On the Day of Judgment he is going to represent everyone, and in fact he already represents them. He represented everyone during the Night Journey and Ascension, when he went through the seven heavens to within two bows-lengths of the Divine Presence.[9]

So when you look at *YaSeen,* you see *Ya* which is the last letter of the alphabet (the 28the letter). Because of its position of being the last letter, *Ya* is the seal of the Arabic alphabet. And because knowledge is transmitted through words and words are composed of letters, the letter *Ya* represents the whole of knowledge based on the Arabic alphabet. The Qur'an is God's Ancient Words expressed through the Arabic alphabet, from *Alif*, the first letter, to *Ya,* the last. Therefore the Prophet ﷺ is the beginning and he is the end.

God mentioned that the Prophet ﷺ is the Seal of the prophets. What is the meaning of that saying, 'Seal of the Prophets' or 'Seal of Prophecy?' The word in Arabic for 'seal,' *khatim,* when varied slightly, means 'end,' *khatm.*

A seal shows the end. Why do you go to a notary public? To seal what you have written, or to authenticate it. So the Prophet ﷺ authenticates for everyone. He has to authenticate what every

---

[9] C.f. *And [he] was at a distance of but two bow-lengths or (even) nearer;* Suratu 'n-Najm (The Star), 53:9.

previous prophet did. Can you authenticate anyone whom you do not know? No. You must know them and you must have witnessed what they did. How can the Prophet ﷺ authenticate what others have done if he was not present in the time of every other prophet?

Therefore he is the one who accompanied all prophets, and the line of prophets ended with him. He is the end. All the prophets' names are described in the alphabet, so even with all their communities, they cannot enter Paradise without the Prophet ﷺ being a witness over them.

> *How then if We brought from each people a witness, and We brought thee as a witness against these people!*[10]

He is the Witness over mankind, even including prophets. That is the meaning of his being the 'seal.' He authenticates those in front of him. A notary cannot authenticate anything unless you are in his presence. At the grand judgment, the judge must call the witness to give his judgment. God is the best of judges, the Most-Wise among those who are wise. So who is going to be the witness? The Seal of Messengers ﷺ. He has to witness on Adam ﷺ which means he was with Adam ﷺ.

Future Knowledge

The second letter is *Seen*.

Seen in Arabic represents the future. Any word that begins with *Sin* is in the future. *Sanureehim, sayakunu, sawfa, sanaktubu.* Prophet ﷺ is the seal of what came before him (by *Ya*) and he is the seal of what is in future (by *Seen*) until Judgment.

"*Sawfa yakun,*" translated as,

---

[10] Suratu 'n-Nisa (Women), 4:41.

and **_soon will come the inevitable_**.[11]

The verse, **_Wa la-sawfa_** yu'teeka Rabbuka," is translated as:

And **_soon will your Guardian-Lord give you_** (O Muhammad), that wherewith you shalt be well-pleased.[12]

So these two letters indicate the beginning and the future; *Seen* is the future and *Ya* is the end.

That is why the Prophet ﷺ was given such extraordinary eloquence: "I have been given the mother of words"—meaning the ultimate expressiveness in speech. And in another hadith, the Prophet ﷺ said, "I have been given all bodies of knowledge." This hadith means that the Prophet ﷺ was given all the words—comprehensively. Prophet ﷺ also said, "I have received the Keys of the Unseen, except for five."[13] The Prophet ﷺ, when he went on the Night Journey and Ascension, was granted by God the "Knowledge of the Firsts and the Lasts."

With all this, it is not voluntary to love him—you are obliged to love him.

How happy are you to take your son to marry? It is the best time. That is because you love him. If that kind of love goes to the Prophet ﷺ, everything in your life will change. Try to meditate on these two letters, *Ya* and *Seen* and understand them and try to open them and research them. You will find that God will open to your heart knowledge that no one knows and that is not recorded in books, knowledge from our shaykh, Mawlana Shaykh Muhammad Nazim Adil al-Haqqani, may God give him long life.

---

[11] Suratu 'l-Furqan (The Criterion), 25:77.
[12] Suratu 'd-Duha (Forenoon), 93:5.
[13] Ibn Hajar, *Fath al-Bari* (Dar al-Fikr ed. 1:124 and 8:514).

When the name of Muhammad ﷺ is inscribed in a circle one sees the form of man, the *Meem* representing the head, the arms and the legs making a perfect circle balanced in the middle.

The Honored Man.

YaSeen

By the Qur'an, full of Wisdom;[14]

The Prophet's ﷺ name is mentioned, followed by the Qur'an.

Similarly, the Chapter *TaHa* ﷺ is structured the same way, for *TaHa* is also a name of the Prophet ﷺ. The chapter *TaHa* begins with,

TaHa [15]

This is followed by the verse,

We have not sent down the Qur'an to you to cause you distress,[16]

In the Chapter the Night of Power, al-Qadr, we find that the Prophet ﷺ is mentioned with the Qur'an.

We have indeed revealed this (Message) in the Night of Power:[17]

The words "Night of Power" are mentioned three times in this chapter. There is a fourth reference to "Night of Power" in the last verse, because the word "this" in it refers to the Night of Power.

Peace!...This (night) is until the rise of morn![18]

---

[14] Surah YaSeen, 36:1-2.
[15] Surah TaHa, 20:1.
[16] Surah TaHa, 20:2.
[17] Suratu 'l-Qadr (The Night of Decree), 97:1.

That makes four references in total to the "Night of Power." Those words in Arabic are composed of seven letters. So we have this seven-lettered phrase occurring four times: 7 x 4 = 28—the number of letters of the alphabet, meaning all 28 letters of the alphabet were given with the Qur'an, when it was revealed as a whole on that night.

The Qur'an is made up of 28 letters.

And the Prophet ﷺ said, "*YaSeen* is the heart of the Qur'an." And we see it was revealed in one night. The letter *Ya,* last in the alphabet, concludes all the letters of those composing the Qur'an.

The Prophet ﷺ said that chapter *YaSeen* is the heart of the Qur'an, and that all the knowledge is included in that first letter of the name. That gives us an indication of how important it is to study the Qur'an.

Why are we all gathered here? To celebrate the memorization of the Qur'an. Are we happy? Yes. So what do you think when God taught the Prophet ﷺ the Holy Qur'an. Was he not happy also?

We are wasting time. The entire Community of Prophet ﷺ is wasting its time.

I will give a hadith on that issue.

Seen is the last letter of this one of Prophet's ﷺ names. Anything that indicates the future in Arabic begins with *Seen*.

Soon will We show them (sanureehim) *our Signs...*[19]

Everything that begins in the future is started with *Seen*.

---

[18] Suratu 'l-Qadr (The Night of Decree), 97:5.
[19] Surah Fussilat (Elucidated), 41:53.

God gave the Prophet ﷺ the knowledge of 'the Firsts and the Lasts'. Therefore to study the Holy Qur'an means to study all things.

Those who are far from understanding Islam, and those who are not following the *sunnah* of the Prophet ﷺ, are in innovation, and under God's punishment, despite their attempts to apply the hadith "all innovations are misguidance and all misguidance is in the Fire," against traditional Islam and Muslims.

Among the signs of the Last Days are that the number of leaders will increase, and more people will be reciting Qur'an, but they recite it quickly without memorizing or understanding; fewer scholars will exist and people will study secular sciences instead of religion; and when many people have memorized the Qur'an but few have delved deeply into it. He said it would be a time when people chase after this worldly life and there will be a great turmoil and trials, and people's money and possessions will increase. People will skim through the Qur'an—like they do today, when they are looking for something specific—even including unbelievers. People will recite the Qur'an in mosques, and when they see that no one is following it, they will retreat to their homes to make mosques in their homes.

Today we see too many leaders and too many reciters of Qur'an, who open the Qur'an to read it quickly without taking the time and care to memorize it and study it external and internal meanings. Now, hiding behind the Internet everyone has become a mufti[20] and is 'teaching' about Islam.

May God forgive us and be pleased with our host's family.

---

[20] Mufit: a scholar qualified through intensive study and training, to make legal rulings in Islamic Law (Shari'ah).

WATCH AFTER YOUR TRUST

This trust we must not lose—we must return it whence it came. If you have money in your pocket or something valuable, and you are walking with people, you will always try to see if you lost it. Do you have your credit cards? Check your credit cards.

When you are on ʿumrah[21] or hajj, and you are wearing the special clothes of hajj[22], and you are making circumambulation around the Kaʿbah to complete the first condition of your hajj or ʿumrah.[23] During your circumambulation, there are not hundreds of people there—rather there are hundreds of thousands of people, is that not right? And all of them are doing circumambulation at the same time. You are inside this crowd, and your heart must be where at this moment? With Allah. Why have you gone there? For your afterlife.

Have you been there yet? No? Next year, God willing.

So your heart must focus on what you have gone there for—for God. And Satan comes, saying, "Be careful, be careful, the one beside you will pull your money, check to make sure you have the money." You begin to check, thinking, "Are my things still there or did I lose them?"

---

[21] A shorter version of hajj that can be performed at any time of the year, not only during the hajj time period.
[22] *ihram*, which is made from two sheets, any kind of sheets, that are not sewn.
[23] after the intention of purity for pilgrimage and a shower (*ghusl*) and then wearing the *ihram* and praying two cycles of prayer.

Who checked their money during circumambulation? Anyone? [Yes.] How many times did you check? Did you check?

Did anyone check? All of us checked, to prevent a thief from coming with a razor—the thieves are very clever there; they come with razors and cut, take and run, very quickly—so what do you do? You are constantly checking, always putting your hand on your money.

Some people are more clever—they give whatever they have to hold to the women who are with them, because the women can wear clothes that are stitched. And then they form a circle around the women in order that the women cannot be attacked.

Therefore they have tried to think, to use their minds in order to protect their money.

You are worried about losing the money, which is alright. Are you not worried to lose the trust with which God has entrusted you? God trusted you:

> *We did indeed offer the Trust to the heavens and the earth and the mountains; but they refused to undertake it, being afraid thereof: but man undertook it;- He was indeed unjust and foolish;*[24]

He said, "We have extended the trust to the heavens and mountains and earth to carry it, but they said, 'No our Lord, please, we cannot.'"

Who agreed to carry the trust of this verse? Mankind. "You were an oppressor to yourself; you do not know your limits."

Not all were ignorant oppressors. Those who were not oppressors took responsibility for receiving that soul that He gave us—that living power that comes from Himself.

---

[24] Suratu 'l-Ahzab (The Confederates), 33: 72.

> *To God We belong, and to Him is our return;*[25]
>
> *Among the Believers are men who have been true to their covenant with Allah. Of them some have completed their vow (to the extreme), and some (still) wait: but they have never changed (their determination) in the least;*[26]

Some kept it clean. They were described as "men" who kept their Covenant and their Trust—trustworthy people, *as-sadiqeen*. When they said something they kept it.

As we are checking our money, and we are checking it in the Ka'bah, we have to check our soul there, that is more valuable. We are there but are we thinking of this world or of the next life.

We are still thinking of this world even when we are in a very holy, sacred place.

If we are worried for money, what about when God calls us and asks us what we have done?

> *(Then) shall each soul know what it has sent forward and (what it has) kept back.* [27]

We have an account, a credit account and a debit account – the right is the credit account. Left is the debit account.

"The people of the Right Hand." God likes the right. Leftists, *"the people of the Left Hand,"* are destined for the fire. That is even mentioned in the Holy Qur'an—rightists and leftists are mentioned in the Holy Qur'an. That was mentioned 1,400 years ago.

---

[25] Suratu 'l-Baqara (The Heifer), 2:156.
[26] Suratu 'l-Ahzab (The Confederates), 33:23.
[27] Suratu 'l-Infitar (The Cleaving), 82:5.

Did you read that in the Qur'an?

God said:

> *The Companions of the Left Hand, - what will be the Companions of the Left Hand? (They will be) in the midst of a Fierce Blast of Fire and in Boiling Water.*[28]

Communists are going to be asked what they have done. God likes everything right, on the "right path." The word "right" has a double meaning in Arabic as it does in English, meaning both the "right side" and the "correct side."

So are we checking for the day when God is going to ask us? On the right side He put the credits, the good, and on the left side, debits, danger, red. Leftists are always dangerous. Do not listen to them—leftists, socialists, communists. They are always wrong. Even if they appear correct, and you think they are right, they are wrong.

Be from the "people of the right," as the angels who write the good actions are from the right, and the angels who write the bad actions are on the left. Do not let your debits to be too much. Then they eat away your credits.

You are at the Ka'bah, you left your children, your family and your wealth. You left everything to go for hajj or 'umrah (perhaps during Ramadan). Many people go for 'umrah during Ramadan. If you went for showing off, it is not going to be a sincere trip. Similarly if you are going and you waste what you have donated by making all kinds of problems there, by fighting and argument and anger, then do not go.

Really you should go, but do not waste your trip. Go for God, and keep that trip.

---

[28] Suratu 'l-Waqi'a (The Event), 56:41.

So as we are worried not to lose our passports and money, always checking ourselves, so must we always check our self: did I lose the trust that God gave me on the day of God's saying to us, before this life in the World of Souls, "Am I not your Lord?"²⁹ You have to keep that promise in mind. Sincerity is what God wants.

*Fear God, be pious, and then He will teach you.*³⁰

You [to a specific person in the audience] are studying Arabic to learn. And you also. And you what are you studying? Nothing. You are studying to be a doctor, or an engineer or whatever. For what? For this world—is that not right? Is that for the afterlife? No, it is not. For the afterlife is: *"fear God, be pious, and then He will teach you."*

Look at the example of Sayyidina Khidr ﷺ.

*We taught him from our heavenly knowledge.*³¹

Sayyidina Khidr ﷺ is pious. Some scholars consider him to be a prophet while others consider him to be a saint, a *wali*, a Friend of God.

God gave us this world in which to live. When you study to be doctor or an engineer, a lawyer, an artist, or any other profession and you keep your piety and balance your life; then you are on the right side and it is accepted to work for this life. But if you are forgetting the afterlife, that is something different.

If you are learning "secular" science, and you have piety, then God will inspire your heart. Then when you learn in this world and spend in His way, by raising your children correctly and educating them in God's Way—which means education, helping

---

²⁹ Suratu 'l-'Araaf (The Heights), 7:172.
³⁰ Suratu 'l-Baqara (The Heifer), 2:282.
³¹ Suratu 'l-Kahf (The Cave), 18:65.

your community and helping your country, then God will give you heavenly knowledge. Then God will describe you in the verse:

> *Among the Believers are men who have been true to their covenant with Allah.* [32]

> *O you who believe! Fear God and be with those who are true (in word and deed).* [33]

You cannot be one of those described in this verse as *"true (in word and deed),"* but you can be sincere and accompany one who is. If you are not sincere you cannot accomplish that. If you are insincere, then you are on a different way than them. If you are sincere, you can accompany them; they work and their hearts are with Allah, they are remembering their Lord. There are a lot of people like that.

This world is going. How long are you going to live? One day they will say, *"salaam 'alaykum—peace unto you!"* and you will go from this life. You are not going to take anything except your deeds. Your nice possessions you will be left behind you.

May God guide us to the right way, to good actions in His Way and in the Way of the Prophet ﷺ and in the Way of Islam.

And in the end my advice to myself and to you is that this is a difficult time. Do not involve yourself in any political issue. Keep to yourself. As I mentioned the *hadith* in yesterday's Friday Prayer sermon, "Keep to yourself." Do not bother with anyone else. You do not know for sure who is your friend and who is not. Keep to your family and to your children; to God and to His Prophet ﷺ. Because now is a time of too much darkness and too many problems. You cannot change anything.

---

[32] Suratu 'l-Ahzab (The Confederates), 33:23.
[33] Suratu 't-Tawbah (The Repentance), 9:119.

Say, "God, my Lord, You know what is best for the people of Islam."

The Preciousness of the Prophet's Blood

Every meeting—every time—we sit and meet and then we separate. After every meeting there is a separation. After every separation you do not know whether or not there will be another meeting.

A meeting can be for five minutes and then there is a separation. Or we may sit for one hour and then there is a separation. Or we may sit for one year, but then, always, there is a separation. Even if we sit for fifty years, there will be a separation at the end. We may sit for seventy years—but at the end there is a separation.

That means your life. You were sent by God to meet the actions that you are going to do. As soon as that series of actions ends, your life ends.

When whatever God has written for your lifespan ends, there is then no longer any meaning to your staying. And that is why what is important for us to do in this world is to achieve good actions by following what we learned from the Prophet ﷺ of God's Orders.

When life comes to an end what God has assigned to you as your job is over. It means you are going to leave that job—you will be fired. They use a technical term: laid off. Finished.

So laying you off, when your series of actions is finished, means no more work for you in this world. God takes back your soul, which is what enabled you to live in this body.

To achieve the actions that God gave to you, He has to give you a vehicle—your body—which will enable you to do the task assigned to you on this earthly plane. As we have explained before, among all the planets why is Earth the only one able to sustain life? Here you have water, life, air, warmth, shade, every kind of element that makes life possible.

Why is there no life on the moon? Why not on Venus? Why not on the sun?

And it is God's wisdom that wanted this earth to be the vehicle, the space shuttle of this universe that can accommodate the life of human beings.

A Touch of Paradise

After Satan whispered to Adam ﷺ in Paradise, he was ordered by God to descend from the heavens. God sent him down. Where did He send him? He sent him to a place we call Planet Earth.

If God had sent him to Mars, Mars would be habitable—Mars would have been Planet Earth.

As soon as he touched earth, this world became able to sustain life.

As we explained in the commentary on the Chapter of the Sun[34] and the Chapter of the Cleaving,[35] when you have a wild tree and you want the tree to bear fruit, you can accomplish that by grafting the wild tree onto a fruitful tree. What will happen? When you graft a wild tree with a fruitful tree, the grafted wild tree becomes a fruitful tree.

---

[34] Suratu '
[35] Suratu 'l-,

So if planet Earth was wild like Mars; when Adam ﷺ put his feet on Earth, feet which had been touching Paradise, from the mere traces of Paradise that were on his feet, the whole Earth was transformed into a living planet able to sustain life.

Look at the universe. There is no place like this one with rivers, snow, jungles, deserts, and wilderness—everything. Here it is like Paradise. If there were no sins here, it would be like a perfect Paradise.

And God described Paradise as full of rivers, mountains, trees and food—as having whatever you desire—even rivers of wine. Is it not so? [Yes.]

So that was only in Paradise. Look through the universe—there is no such place. Why only Earth? Because it is a graft from Paradise that came on the traces of Adam's feet.

God gave to us in this environment a lifespan in which we can achieve whatever is possible of good actions—or bad—that is up to us. When this time-frame for achieving that is finished, there is no longer any need to stay. Then they say "Come, God is calling you."

That is why the Prophet (s) ﷺ said, "The deeds of man will be cut off except for three: a flowing donation, knowledge from which people benefit, or a pious child who prays for [the person who died]."

So when your actions are cut, what happens? You die.

God gave you that soul as a trust in a time prior to this worldly existence, in the World of Souls.[36] It is like when you want a loan. You say to your friend "can you loan me this?" He says, "Yes. Just return it to me as you got it." You take it and at the end

---

[36] Arabic: ʿAlam al-arwah.

you return it. You agree on how long and the condition. It is a trust.

So God says, "How long do you want? I am giving it to you for seventy years. I will see how you do."

The other one is given twenty years, another seventy years, another sixty years, another ten years, another is given five years. When that allotted timeframe is finished you go.

That is a separation. Separation from your achievement. You go to another meeting, the life of the grave. That will be in a different style and a different condition. You will be living and the Prophet ﷺ described part of it: "Either your grave will be a ditch from the ditches of Hell, or a piece of Paradise."

It depends whether you kept that soul that God gave you clean or not. If you kept it clean they send it to a clean area. Do not think when they put you down, underground, that narrow trench is the area you will inhabit. No, God will change it completely.

Just like the mirage in the desert; you see water, and for you it <u>is</u> water. You need strong eyes to distinguish a mirage from real water.

Because we are in this world, God does not show reality to us for these eyes are fake and cannot see. You need strong vision, good eyes to know the reality of what you are seeing.

You see the grave as a hole in the dirt. In reality if God wants to change it to a Paradise, He will change it. If He wants to change it to a pit of fire, He will change it.

It depends on how we carry the trust that God has given us—and all of us are falling into that ditch of Satan, running after Satan and not running after God and his Prophet ﷺ, because of the bad desires our ego is dragging us into. That is why the

Prophet ﷺ was always saying to the Companions after they returned from fighting in a war of self-defense:

> We are returning from the lesser struggle to the greater struggle (against our selves).

If we are not going to be fighting our ego's bad desires we are never going to reach a successful moment.

The Gift of Forgiveness

> In the hadith we mentioned in the Friday Prayer sermon today, the Prophet ﷺ was sitting with the Companions, and laughed suddenly. And Sayyidina 'Umar ؓ asked, "Ya Rasulullah can you tell us why you are laughing?"
>
> He explained, "Allah showed me two people coming, and they are being taken for account on Judgment Day. One was an oppressor and the other one was oppressed by him."
>
> At the end—we will not go into the hadith—Allah tells the oppressor, "I will take from the good deeds of the oppressor to give to the oppressed." And still the oppressed wanted more because the oppressor's good deeds were not enough to cover what was due him [for what he had done to him of oppression]. And he had nothing left to give to him, no more good deeds. Then he said, "OK, I give from my sins for him to carry."
>
> And what was left after that? Nothing. Then when there was nothing left to give or take, God said, "Raise your head, and look." He looked up and saw so many cities made from silver and palaces from gold, ornamented with pearls. That man asked "Is this is for a prophet, trustworthy one, or a martyr?"

God said, "No, this is for the one who has the price." He asked, "O my Lord, what is the price?" God said, "You have the price." The man said, "O my Lord, I do not have anything." God then says, "No you have the price—if you forgive your brother you will own all this and take him with you into your Paradise."

Why are we in all these problems we see today? Because we are not trying to forgive and bring people together. Instead what are we doing? Fighting? Fighting for what? For this world.

Holy Blood

When the Prophet ﷺ was at the Battle of Uhud, and the unbelievers were fighting the Muslims and trying to conquer them, and the Muslims were defending themselves, the Prophet's ﷺ teeth were broken in the battle and blood was coming from that wound.

And God said, "O Gabriel, in the quickest way that you can, catch that blood." And Gabriel عليه السلام said, "I was never ordered such an order that I had to move so quickly as when I had to move in order to catch that blood from hitting the ground. If the blood had fallen to the ground there would have been nothing left living on this earth."

That is our evidence that when Sayyidina Adam عليه السلام came, the earth was dry and lifeless, and when he put his feet on the earth, feet which were covered with traces of Paradise, it turned this earth into a form of Paradise.

If the blood of the Prophet ﷺ had touched the earth, all life would have been removed from earth and it would have dried up—just like Mars.

No reward do I ask of you for this except the love of those near of kin.[37]

I am not exaggerating. God is telling the Prophet ﷺ to say, "I am not asking anything from you except to take care of my family."

When Sayyidina al-Hassan ؓ and Sayyidina al-Husayn ؓ came to the Prophet ﷺ, he used to put them on his back, and move around; playing with them—and the Prophet ﷺ informed his Companions that they were going to be killed.

What were they fighting for? Those who are fighting for this world killed the grandchildren of the Prophet ﷺ. They were fighting for what? For this world. For leadership.

His blood was dripping in the streets of that land when they killed him.

His blood had been dripping—blood which came from the Prophet ﷺ through Fatima ؓ and from Sayyidina 'Ali ؓ, and both were from the Family of the Prophet ﷺ, Sayyidina 'Ali ؓ being the son of his uncle Abu Talib.

Where that blood was dripping, disruption constantly comes. That is why people throughout history encountered many problems in that region. We are not speaking of any government or leadership—but Sayyidina al-Husayn's ؓ blood was spilled there.

For Sayyidina Muhammad ﷺ God ordered, "Take it away." [i.e. prevent his holy blood from being spilled on earth.] That was for His Prophet ﷺ. For the grandchildren of the Prophet ﷺ it was allowed in fact to spill there. Therefore throughout all the years of history there have been problems there at various times.

---

[37] Suratu 'sh-Shura (The Consultation), 42:23.

The Prophet ﷺ pointed to the East and said, "Tribulations will come from there, from where the side of the head of Satan comes out."[38] And he said, "The Hour will not be established till a fire come out of the land of Hijaz, and it will throw light on the necks of the camels at Basra." [39]

So we go back and say we have to fix ourselves. If we do not fix ourselves… Everything that creates problem today is from love of this world. Husbands and wives fight for what? Love of this world. Children and parents fight for this world. Brother against brother, sister against sister.

Why do they fight? If it were for the afterlife, they would not fight. Do you see anyone fighting to be first in the afterlife before you—they do not care? "You take this and I take this." God tested Sayyidina Adam ؏, whenArchangel Gabriel came in the form of a man and hid himself on earth by the order of Allah. Adam ؏ spied him and said, "You are here?" and Gabriel ؏ said, "You are here. There are two of us." Adam ؏ said, "No we are three. I have my wife. We have to divide the earth between ourselves." And after discussion, it turned to argument and finally into a wrestling match.

From the beginning that was the story. Recall how Abel was killed by Cain. Abel was generous. When asked to give something in the Way of God, he gave his best sheep to his Lord, and the other gave his worst. When Abel's sacrifice was accepted by God and Cain's was not, Cain killed his brother in a jealous rage.[40]

---

[38] Bukhari.
[39] Bukhari.
[40] C.f. Suratu 'l-Ma'idah (The Table Spread), 5:27.

It is better when we throw love of this world from our hearts—at that time you are able to have a lot of money for it will not be an issue that holds you back from worship and obligations.

Both the old and the young, we have to teach our children and ourselves what we have to look forward to: "You alone, O our Lord; our Prophet ﷺ; our Islam." If we achieve that we will achieve everything.

May God guide us to the way of Prophet ﷺ, the way that God wanted for us; to the way of his Companions ؈ and of His saints.

WARS OF THE LAST DAYS

[Question: how do we see the future? Are there signs through which we can learn something and get guidance from?]

The Prophet ﷺ did not leave anything without explaining it. Do we believe in that or not? [Yes.] So he showed us what is *halal*, permitted, and what is *haram*, forbidden. Do we believe in that or not? [Yes.]

He explained what is going to happen in his time, after his time and in the time where everything is going to end in an era before the Judgment. Do we believe in that or not? Yes.

So since we believe in that, speaking from an Islamic or a religious perspective, and since we believe in the Prophet ﷺ, and in Islam, then we have to take into consideration what the Prophet ﷺ said.

We cannot take into consideration what world leaders are saying—because world leaders are not spiritual leaders. The spiritual leader and Seal of Messengers is Sayyidina Muhammad ﷺ. What did he say? The Prophet ﷺ said that this world is not going to last forever. And as Muslims, one of our beliefs is in Judgment Day—that this world will not last forever.

We believe Judgment Day is coming. Recall the famous hadith narrated by Sayyidina 'Umar ؓ.

Archangel Gabriel ؑ asked Sayyidina Muhammad, "When is the Judgment Day." The Prophet ﷺ replied, "The one that was asked does not know more that the one who is asking."⁴¹

It means "You and I do not know." But if God wants the prophets to know, He will give them that knowledge. And as traditional Muslims, we believe that God gave Prophet Muhammad ﷺ the knowledge from beginning to end, but that he had no permission to mention all of what he knew.

But the Prophet ﷺ did list the Signs of the Last Days. He put the scene before us. As events are happening, as mentioned by the Prophet ﷺ, it means that time is coming to an end.

When the Prophet ﷺ says something, we have to focus on what he predicted. It is not that we do not know and we are still guessing. The Prophet ﷺ described what is going to happen.

The fact is, we did not achieve what is needed for the hereafter and we did not try to learn the faith, because our hope is to live longer and to enjoy a very fancy lifestyle.

The Prophet ﷺ was one day with one of his Companions. He asked him, "You are not a stranger, come with me to my daughter's house." He went with him and the Prophet ﷺ knocked on the door of Sayyida Fatima ؇. She asked, "Who is there?" He said, "I and a man, who is not of your near kin." She said, "I do not have anything to cover me except a robe of Sayyidina 'Ali, and I have nothing to put on my head."

The Prophet ﷺ said, "Wear it and I will give you something to put on your head."

Then she said, "O my father. I am very hungry. Since yesterday I have had nothing in my stomach."

---

⁴¹ Bukhari.

He said, "O my daughter, be patient. For three days I did not have anything in my stomach, and I have married you to someone who resembles no one in this world."

So this is the Prophet ﷺ; the one that God described in all Qur'an and in all hadith and raised his name with His name and described him as the "best of creation." And he had eaten nothing for three days. Why? Because his message to us and to the Companions is for the afterlife—for the next life.

They suffered, not eating for three days at a time. They suffered and were patient.

We Muslims, in general, as a community, most of our desires are not in line with the Prophet's ﷺ desires or with the desires of his Companions. We are looking to this world more than towards the afterlife. So when you focus more on this world, then all these predictions that the Prophet ﷺ foretold are no longer of value to you. You do not consider them.

You might look at hadith on how to pray, how to fast and to make hajj, because all of those are your obligations in this world—when you look at the hadith of the Prophet ﷺ relating to performing additional worship, or relating to the afterlife, your interest may be lacking. And the Prophet ﷺ has explained much of what is going to happen, but we have closed our eyes and ears and do not want to see it.

Now you are asking, of course, for this world. The Prophet ﷺ was sent to this world for a time less than this—pointing to his two fingers. He said, "I was sent close to Judgment Day as these two fingers." [42]

---

[42] Bukhari.

We Muslims are still seeing the end as far away, and yet it is close. Still we continue making programs and plans for years and decades into the future.

Whatever you are going to do, I am sorry to say, you are going to die. Whether you live hungry or not, you are going to die. Whether you eat plain bread or fine meals, you are still going to die.

So the importance is not how much wealth we have, or what we eat, but how much is enough. To be content and satisfied with what God gave to you. To be content is what we have to look forward to with our eyes.

You can find in India, or in Malaysia, someone sitting on top of a mountain—living in a hut and happy, living for sixty or seventy years. He is happy with his life, while someone living in a palace, with people all around him may or not be happy. But in both cases both are going to die.

Imam Ghazzali ق said, "What is important is how content is person with what God gave him." When someone is happy with what God gave him, of course he will think, "What must I do for the afterlife?" At that time he will receive more information on what is coming day by day.

The Prophet ﷺ said, "There will come a time when all the countries of the world will come against you to destroy you."

It is a problem with you. Not just with Muslims, but a problem with Islam. Because you cannot play with Islam—it is the complete and perfect religion. Like other religions, today they are changing even Islam.

Last week I was looking for a mosque and we passed by a church. I never saw such a thing. The speakers were so loud you could hear them from the street. And I was peeking inside and people were chanting and they had so many people on the drums, with violins and piano, all this! And there inside, you could see the men and women dancing and huffing and puffing, completely hysterical, and some of them were comforting the others.

In Islam you cannot do that. You cannot say, "I want to modernize Islam." That is a problem.

The Prophet ﷺ said, "Nations will come against you."

Sayyidina 'Umar ؓ asked, "Are we fewer than the others at that time?" Prophet ﷺ said, "No! You will be great in numbers, but with no voice. You will be as nothing, you will be weak, unable to do anything." He described the situation that the community of the Prophet ﷺ is seeing with their very eyes today.

Show me if the Muslims can do anything! Look at the Arab summits, where the leaders spend their time cursing each other. These are the leaders of the Muslims!

Prophet ﷺ described that situation when he said, "I made three supplications to God, two of which He accepted and the last He refused. I asked for my community not to be destroyed by earthquakes, floods or plagues. He said, 'Yes.' This is the first part. And second, I asked that my nation not be destroyed root and branch. And He said, 'Yes.' Finally I asked that the community not fall to fighting each other. And for that request, God said, 'No, I will test them by their fighting with one another.'"[43]

Now they are fighting each other. Before, during the Ottoman time, Muslims were working together. Also before, during the

---

[43] A similar tradition is related in Malik's *al-Muwatta*.

time of the Abbasids and Ummayad sultanates, Muslims did not fight amongst themselves as much.

So now we have sixty or more nations.

The Prophet ﷺ said, "Judgment Day will not come about until two large groups fight each other."

What we are seeing today is that there are two camps forming in the world.

Grandshaykh said that, from the spiritual side, 98% of the signs of the coming of Sayyidina Mahdi ؑ and Prophet Jesus ؑ have taken place. Only 2% are left. The first he said that all the Arab and Muslim countries would be aligned with America and they will solve the Palestinian problem. And he said "There would be a big war." If we look behind us a short way, we see that most of the Arab leadership sided with America. Did anyone oppose America?

So, most of the Arab countries are following America. Then he said, "There will be a fight between America and the Eastern countries."

And America is from the west. And Mawlana used to say, "Bani Asfar [will fight] Russia and these countries. There will be a fight between these two big parties."

In the past it was Russia against the United States. Now we see a change, but there remain two main blocs. In any event, in accordance with our belief in that hadith, it is going to happen. Before Judgment Day there will be a war between two large groups.

And it will end up in Turkey, in the valley of Umuq, near Iskenderun where there is a big plain. He said, "From the immensity of that war the flow of the blood from the people who have been killed, would be strong enough to move a calf just as it would in a river."

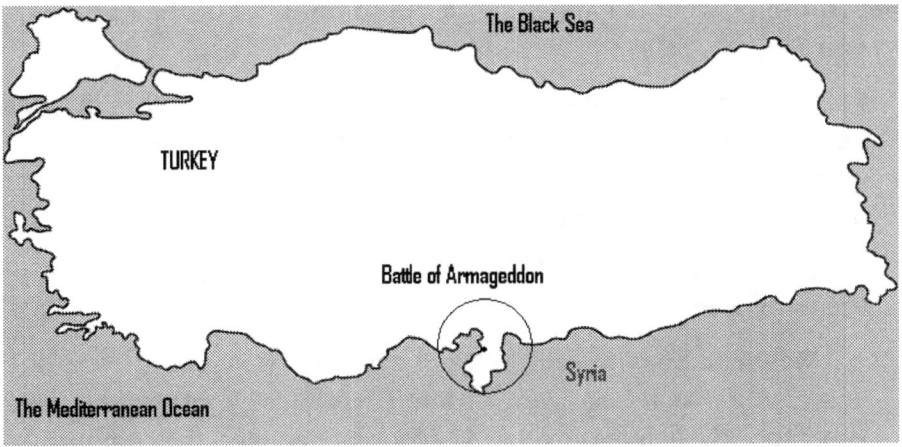

That means there will be a very great war, which all holy books predict: Armageddon.

At that time Sayyidina Mahdi ﷺ and Prophet Jesus ﷺ will be given permission to appear. So that is what we are looking for today and seeing—that is what is happening.

The Prophet ﷺ said, "A fire will emerge from the land of the Hijaz due to which the camels of Basra will run from its intense heat."

And how many traditions are there on the Last Days? I was showing them yesterday, there were six volumes. They have been put together, describing the entire situation.

From where we are there is no way to go back to peace. Every day is more dangerous than before. Do not expect that this world is going to go along peacefully and end peacefully. It is not in the hands of anyone. It is in the hands of the Prophet ﷺ, to whom God gave authority, who then put it in hands of saints.

An enormous amount of fornication is happening now, and an enormous amount of homosexuality—like the people of Lot—that is happening also. Homosexuality is everywhere now, even in Muslim countries. That is making God's revenge come quickly, because of what is happening in the community of the Prophet ﷺ now.

So saints now have their hands tied. Although all is in their hands—God gave them authority but not the permission to change what is happening. Some saints want it to happen quickly. But it is moving forward. But do not worry.

God said to Sayyidina Musa ؑ, "I am going to destroy Pharaoh soon."

Mawlana Shaykh said, "When every saint is dying, each one possessing a secret, Sayyidina Mahdi ؑ is taking that secret." This is because the saints prevent the action of Satan on the community of the Prophet ﷺ. As these saints are dying, there is no substitute for them, so their power is less and less. Before you could see saints everywhere; now you cannot see them anywhere. Now the power has been taken, and it is all in hands of the Prophet ﷺ.

We feel we are very near to a huge catastrophe of explosive events in this world. An catastrophe of such magnitude that it will change history as we know it. Saints are not expecting this world to last more than fifty years. That is something we cannot understand. That is coming up and we are going to see it and our children will see it. This world cannot take more than fifty years.

> There is a hadith, recorded in the Quranic commentary, *Ruh al-Bayan*, in explaining the Chapter of Time (Suratu 'l-'Asr) in which the Prophet ﷺ said, "My nation will live, while good, for one day, and while bad, for half a day," and then he recited: '*Verily a Day in the sight of thy Lord is like a thousand years of your reckoning.*' [22:4]"

The Prophet ﷺ did not relate only 400 hadith. Even Imam Bukhari recorded 4,000. There were many traditions, but of different particular application. There were some hadith that were called weak, although they might have been correct. And the saints asked the Prophet ﷺ directly about some traditions when they were present with him. Many saints through their visions asked the Prophet ﷺ about traditions they were concerned about.

And Grandshaykh was in seclusion for five years completely alone, eating only seven olives a day and one piece of bread. And in one vision, he saw the Prophet ﷺ and asked about the hadith of 1,500 years. The Prophet ﷺ said, "Yes, that is true." That means if a saint asks the Prophet ﷺ if a hadith is correct, that is accepted in Islam.

Now if we take that hadith of the Prophet ﷺ, that the community of Prophet ﷺ has 1,500 years, we are now in year 1424, so what are we expecting? That is from the *Hijri* calendar. If we add the 13 years of Madinah before the *hijra*, we are now in the year 1440 after Prophet ﷺ came. 1,500 minus 1,440 equals 60 years. So saints are not expecting more than that.

So, slow down, and do more for your afterlife. And do not play too much. It is better. If you are happy with what God gave to you, then praise belongs to God, that is better.

[I have a short question.]

This is a western style, to ask questions.

[While you were talking, I have been thinking—how will we recognize Mahdi ﷺ, and how will we not be fooled by The Antichrist?]

Do not worry. I am not going to go into that, but since you recognized Mawlana Shaykh Nazim ق easily, Sayyidina Mahdi ﷺ will be recognized far more easily.

Grandshaykh said, "Anyone with a seed of faith in his heart will hear the calling of 'Allahu Akbar' by al-Mahdi ﷺ from East to West."

At that time you must make the effort to move, either to Makkah, Madinah, or Damascus. These three cities will be safe. Nowhere else is safe.

You have to carry this world like this [holding a rosary by its tassel]—you see too many threads are in the tassel of these prayer beads? You must only hold it with one thread. But if you are grasping it tightly, it will not fall, it keeps hanging.

There is coming a war from whose intensity no one can predict what will happen.

> *When the Sky is cleft asunder; When the Stars are scattered; When the Oceans are suffered to burst forth; And when the Graves are turned upside down*[44]

When the threads of these prayer bead are going to be cut... What will happen? Everything will fall apart.

Mawlana said, "Out of seven people only one will remain. From seven billion, only one billion will be left. And it will be guided 'missiles' sent by God directly at those that He does not wish to survive the war."

> *Striking them with stones of baked clay*[45]

It is related in the explanation of the Qur'an's Chapter of the Elephant, Suratu 'l-Fil that when the Ka'bah was attacked by the Yemeni King Abraha and his army, Allah sent birds to attack his army. Each bird carried a stone in its beak and two in its claws, and on each "missile" the target's name was written.

---

[44] Suratu 'l-Infitar (The Cleaving), 82:1-4.
[45] Suratu 'l-Fil (The Elephant), 105:4.

There are five different groups of saints with Mahdi: *Budala*, *Nujaba*, *Nuqaba*, *Awtad* and *Akhyar*. These five groups are present with Mahdi ﷺ, behind Mount Qaf.

Qaf; By the Glorious Qur'an.[46]

They are behind that tremendous mountain, which exists outside our earthly plane. Sayyidina Mahdi ﷺ is waiting with these five different groups of saints. Then you there are angels and the believing jinn. They will protect whoever is destined to survive on earth through the expected tribulation. Then at that time, if someone is written to be among the protected ones, even if a bomb falls on his head he will not be killed.

Grandshaykh said, "From the intensity of that war, pieces of the earth will crack apart." Such horrific events are expected. Therefore many saints are trying to postpone it praying, "O my Lord! Not in my time. Not in my time. Let it be in another time."

But it is going to come. So we always ask protection from the time when these atomic bombs are going to fly from one place to another.

[The billion that will be left are before The Antichrist comes?]

When the Antichrist comes he will tour the whole earth.

[And most will go with him?]

Whoever has a seed of faith in his heart and hears the call of Mahdi ﷺ, has to go to Makkah, Madinah or Damascus. And there will be time to move, and those who cannot move, God will give them special power to move by the power of *Bismillah ir-Rahman ir-Raheem*.

---

[46] Surah Qaf. 50:1.

The Antichrist will show Paradise in one hand and Hell in another, and what he will be holding will be the opposite of what they appear to be. So people must not be fooled.

[What about the hadith of the man who will be cut in two, and the Antichrist puts him back together and he says, "You cannot kill me again?"]

Some people say that is Khidr. But he will be one of the sincere Muslims of that time, not Sayyidina Khidr. He is a typical Muslim. It means all Muslims will be like that.

This is the belief of the people of mainstream Islam. People are no longer emphasizing these issues.

[A student relates a dream, where he sees himself seated at table with Mawlana Shaykh Nazim and some ladies. And Mawlana told him, "go and call *Umit Khudree*".]

"*Umit*" is a Turkish word which means "I wish" or "I hope to get that." *Khudree* indicates Sayyidina Khidr. It means "I long for, I hope for, Sayyidina Khidr."

Grandshaykh had a neighbor with twins, Basheer and Nadheer. They would always come to visit. And they were poor. And Mawlana's house was high, on top of a hill so if anything was thrown from the window, it would fall down into a dump.

So one day, Basheer and Nadheer were playing. Grandshaykh liked to slaughter, with his own hands, cows or sheep, from whose meat he would feed the poor and his guests. He liked to cook the intestines but before doing that you have to clean them and cut them—then you put them in soup. So he emptied all the contents of the intestines into a big bucket and he went to the window and dumped it out. And Basheer and Nadheer happened to be playing down below and got drenched with all the contents of the intestines.

Their mother came crying to Grandshaykh because they were very poor, and she did not even have soap with which to wash them. So Mawlana brought them into his home and cleaned them in the bathroom…

So we must continue our struggle.

Yes, the Prophet ﷺ said to continue. You plant. But put your heart with God. Say, "I am giving something in God's way." Give, and God gives you more.

Glory be to God, however much you give, God gives you without any accounting. I have seen that and experienced it. Not only me, but I saw it with many people around Mawlana Shaykh and Grandshaykh. You give and God gives, and if you do not give, you do not receive.

Grandshaykh said that every human being has a chain of provision descending to his head from heaven above. It must always touch his head. If you cut a little bit it comes back to its place—if you cut too much it still comes to its place. So as much as you give in the way of Allah, you receive. Therefore the Prophet ﷺ said, "Wealth is never reduced by charity."

Today all of us are afraid to give. When you close your hand there is no place for someone else to put anything. Our hands are closed tight. Open your hands, then God will send. Therefore struggle as much as you like to do well in this worldly life but always keep in your heart that through your struggling there is always a share for giving in God's Way.

GETTING GOOD GRADES FOR YOUR AFTERLIFE

[Talk in Khalilullah Mosque, Fremont, California]

Islam is a favor you cannot obtain by means of any amount of wealth.

God said:

> *They impress on you (O Muhammad) as a favor that they have embraced Islam. <u>Say, "Count not your Islam as a favor upon me: Nay, God has conferred a favor upon you</u> that He has guided you to the faith, if you be true and sincere.*[47]

Do not think you came to Islam because you did something great. We are only lucky that God granted us to be guided to Islam.

We have to remember that we are weak in God's Presence, weak in our Islamic belief, helpless to do anything that is accepted fully and perfectly or performed in a way that God would accept.

We are praying, all of us, and yet our minds are not in prayer. In such a situation do you believe that is going to be a perfect prayer? So we do our obligations. We do our best but what we are doing is not perfect.

When you have a test, a quiz or an exam in the university and you are studying, you concentrate 100%. When we go to the classroom to take our exam and we have the test in front of us, we

---

[47] Suratu 'l-Hujuraat (The Private Apartments), 49:17.

make our best effort to achieve a perfect grade and we will only be happy if they tell us it is 'A+', 'A' or 'A-.' And in the university, if you are studying to be a doctor or lawyer or whatever, they do not let you in if you do not have good grades. They tell you "Your grades are not high enough to be admitted here."

For example, at Stanford University they look at your grades. What do you have? An 'A?' They say, "We will look at you." If you have an 'A+' they say, "OK, we will take you."

What do you think about Paradise?

There are universities that take even 'D' students, 'A', 'B', 'C', 'D' even 'E'. But they are normal universities, not high-level universities. So if we want to attend a high-level university we must achieve our best.

If we want to be with:

> ...the company of those on whom is the Grace of Allah,- of the Prophets (who teach), the sincere (lovers of Truth), the witnesses (who testify), and the Righteous (who do good): Ah! what a beautiful fellowship![48]

we have to get high 'grades'.

These words are enough for all of us. We do not need more, if we really keep these words in mind. But our minds are shuttered. We look everywhere, in every direction ,but there is no focus.

The Prophet ﷺ, when he said something to the Companions, they would jump to do what he said, struggle for it, each seeking to do it first.

God said:

---

[48] Suratu 'n-Nisa (Women), 4:69.

> *Say (O Muhammad): "If you would love Allah, Follow me: God will love you and forgive you your sins: For God is Oft-Forgiving, Most Merciful."*[49]

God told the Prophet ﷺ to say, "If you really love Allah, then follow me." God said it to the Prophet ﷺ.

Revelation comes in two ways. God is revealing something with the Prophet ﷺ as the addressed person. Here God says, "Say: If you love God then follow me."

Look at the revelation. Usually revelation comes to the Prophet ﷺ to address the people in all their affairs. But in the same revelation this is coming to tell the people to follow Sayyidina Muhammad ﷺ. "Follow me and then God will love you."

It is one verse, but its importance is huge—it covers religion from beginning to end. It means: "If you love Me, follow the Prophet." It did not say "follow Muhammad." Rather it told the Prophet ﷺ to say, *"Follow me!"*

When God addresses someone, He addresses him in the third person, but in this verse he addressed the Prophet ﷺ directly: *"Say!"*

So the Prophet ﷺ came with the message of Islam and ordered us to follow. Now either we follow fully or partially. If we follow partially we will be at a normal level, which is not very special.

If we want to follow correctly or perfectly, then we will be at a higher level. That is why Islam came in three divisions: Islam, Faith (*iman*) and Perfection (*ihsan*). That is why people in the 21st century have been deprived. When they ask us about Islam, we say, "Islam is five pillars." When we speak with Muslims and

---

[49] Surat Aali-'Imraan (The Family of 'Imraan), 3:31.

non-Muslims, everyone repeats the same phrase. Correct? They say, "Islam is this, nothing more," but in reality Islam is not just five pillars. We are leaving out two very great categories.

In addition to the five pillars of Islamic practice, the Prophet ﷺ showed that there are two higher levels: Faith, *Iman*, and Perfected Character, *Ihsan*. The religion is not simply what you are required to do of the five obligations. If you fulfill them you achieve a passing grade. You will go to a university that accepts anyone with a 'D' or an 'E.'

If you want to go to a higher Paradise, no problem. God is saying if you want to go to a higher Paradise, seek to achieve the second division. That is Faith.

> *"The desert Arabs say, "We believe." Say (O Muhammad), "You have no faith; but (only) say, 'We have submitted our wills to Allah,' For Faith has not entered your hearts."*[50]

The Arabs, the Bedouins, said, "We believe." This verse of Qur'an replies to them, "Do not say you entered faith. Only say 'We entered Islam.' Faith has not yet entered your hearts."

Islam you entered—you accepted to do what God asked; you left off associating others with Allah, and you accepted the message of Islam and the message of the Holy Qur'an—so say "we are Muslim," but faith, no. It has not yet entered the heart.

When faith enters the heart, it changes everything. That means you are trying to lift yourself up from 'C' or 'D' grade to a 'B' or an 'A'. That depends on your faith. Some people have very strong faith. Some have it at a middle level, and there are those with faith at a lower level.

---

[50] Suratu 'l-Hujuraat (The Private Apartments), 49:114.

And that is why you see that within the Muslim community people are on different levels. One will have very strong faith, doing his best to push himself to do his best to present Islam. Others do less.

It is not in what you do to show off to people. No. That is politics. You have to show off to God. You have to show how much you will give from your life and your time to worship Him. Not going on TV as a politician and doing an event here or there. Rather it is based on how much sincerity you have in your heart.

The Prophet ﷺ was passing a Companion and said, "Come with me to visit my daughter Fatima," and they went and he knocked on the door. He said, "Open for us, I have one Companion with me."

She said, "O my father I have nothing to cover myself with except a cloth of Sayyidina "Ali." He said, "Cover yourself with it," and he gave her something from his clothes to cover her hair—because a headscarf is important for Muslim women.

We do not want to move into politics but that is where it is going. Nowadays the symbol of a Muslim woman is to take off her headscarf, to become a model: as if the headscarf is not an obligation on our sisters, wives, and mothers—whereas God has stressed it and the Prophet ﷺ mentioned it.

In any case, she covered herself and they entered. The Prophet ﷺ asked, "What do you have to eat?" She said, "By God, my father, I have not had anything since yesterday. I had only one date that I ate."

Look at their sincerity. They were suffering and doing their best. The Prophet's own family was suffering from hunger and yet they were still working for Islam. He ﷺ said, "O my daughter, never mind. For three days I have not had anything to eat."

That is submission to God's Will. Not complaining. We cannot stand to eat less than ten different kinds of food a day, is that not true? If you make an invitation you will have all kinds of different food.

One time a Companion invited the Prophet ﷺ for a meal, and he prepared for a long time for that invitation—as you would prepare when inviting someone important—it takes time.

So that Companion was doing his best, and the day came when Prophet ﷺ entered with his Companions and Abu Bakr as-Siddiq ؓ. They entered and that man said to the Prophet ﷺ, "O Rasulullah, what I have prepared is not enough for your honor." He had been preparing for a long period of time, all kinds of food.

Immediately the Prophet ﷺ pulled his foot back and left saying, "I accept that invitation and my Companions will eat on my behalf." He took Sayyidina Abu Bakr ؓ and left. Sayyidina Abu Bakr ؓ did not say one word.

On his way back, there was a lady who all her life had been praying, "O God accept my prayer to bring the Prophet ﷺ to my door to eat and to see my husband who cannot leave the house due to his illness." She saw the Prophet ﷺ going on his way, and invited him in. She brought him a piece of bread, some water and salt. That bread was very dry, not like today's bread. The Prophet ﷺ put the bread in the water and then put the salt on it. Then he told Abu Bakr, "Eat as if you never ate in your life."

Sayyidina Abu Bakr ؓ was surprised. He said, "O Messenger of Allah! First there was an invitation and you did not eat. And here is water and salt and dry bread and you say to eat as if you never ate in your life?"

The Prophet ﷺ said, "Ya Abu Bakr. Each bite of food contains with it angels which are preparing the food. And when I saw that magnificent table, I saw all those angels and I felt shy from my Lord and I did not touch it. Because we have to accept anything that God gave us, the favor of God is so great upon us, even bread with salt and water."

That is to show how much sincerity the Companions had to God. They did not have love of this world. Today our problem as Muslims is that we are more affected with this worldly life and delaying the importance of our afterlife. That is why when faith enters your heart, it teaches you, "No! Do not forget—there is death."

Faith consists of belief in Allah, His angels, His Books, His Prophets and in the Hereafter, or Judgment Day. Faith reminds of us of death.

The five pillars of Islam are: the testimony of faith, prayer, fasting, charity and pilgrimage—they contain no mention of death.

But the pillars of faith contain mention of the next life—that means we are going to die. So what are you preparing for your death? And the rest of [the testimony of] faith is "... and to believe in destiny, the good and bad of it are from God."

If we are not thinking about death, faith tells us to think about it. It is not just the testimony of faith, prayer, fasting, charity and hajj.

It is, "I **believed** in Allah." Many people pray out of habit. Some pray out of fear of being whipped or beaten. It is not from faith, but from fear. But God does not want us to pray out of fear—rather out of love and sincerity. He (swt) asks us, "Believe in Me and My angels and My Prophets and My books." So what are we believing in from the Holy Qur'an today? Show me?

I will tell you something and some people might be offended but... Many people here are opening the Holy Qur'an and skimming through it. Or perhaps they are leaving it to sit on the shelf. How many people are reading the Qur'an today? Very few. There is no one trying to study the Qur'an.

Our most important goal has become to study secular science. In the past there was no secular knowledge. Studying meant you go for a very intensive course of Shariah, Islamic philosophy and Islamic knowledge of the understanding of the meaning of Qur'an.

It is no longer like that, and there are no more scholars.

'Abdullah bin Amr Ibn al-'As related that the Prophet said:

> God will not take knowledge from the hearts of the scholars but he will take the scholars (they will die and there will be no more to take their places), so people will take extremely ignorant leaders. They will be asked questions and will give legal rulings without knowledge. They are misguided and they misguide others.[51]

Now there are people who have memorized Qur'an, but no real scholars. They did a good job of studying Qur'an but have not read it in depth.

Now faith tells you that you have to study in depth to get an 'A' or 'A+' in the afterlife. Nonetheless, if you are not studying in depth, then you will be kept safe from Hellfire by observing your

---

[51] Bukhari and Muslim.

obligations. But if we believe in the afterlife, and if we truly want to achieve a higher level, then we must study harder.

In the famous Hadith of Gabriel ﷺ, he asked the Prophet ﷺ, "What is moral excellence (or perfection of sincerity)?"

Let us say we achieve faith. Now a 'C' is a passing grade, and even a 'D' is passing. 'E' is 60% and 'F' is failing. Now you want to achieve at least a passing grade, (just to stay on the Straight Path); and how do we achieve higher levels? How do we achieve moral excellence, the level which comes after faith? That is the big question. That is why the four imams studied with guides. Not like today, where everyone calls himself an "imam."

The word 'Imam' means a leader of the Muslims. Yes, there is an imam for a mosque, but if you say that a scholar is an Imam, it means he is the leader of a great school of thought. Before the first leader-imams, there were the Companions, and they were competing in the realm of moral excellence: to worship God "as if seeing Him, and if you are not seeing Him, (and you cannot see Him in this world), at least know He is seeing you."[52]

So how do you say "Allahu Akbar," to begin your prayers, when all your concentration is on, "When am I going to marry" and "how much is in my bank account?" And, "Should I buy the red car or the blue car?"

That is what happens to all of us. As soon as you say "Allahu Akbar!" you must know that God is looking at you. How will you pray then? With what kind of sincerity?

Prophet ﷺ was told in the Chapter of the Cave, Suratu'l-Kahf:

> *And keep your soul (O Muhammad) content with those who call on their Lord morning and evening, seeking*

---

[52] Bukhari.

> <u>His Face</u>; *and let not your eyes pass beyond them,*
> *seeking the pomp and glitter of this Life;*[53]

That means they are asking to be in God's Presence. God was addressing this verse to the Prophet ﷺ. It refers to the the "People of the Bench"[54] who used to sit behind his house—what is now the holy grave of Prophet ﷺ.

In the place of Sayyida Fatima's ؓ extension, there is a bench where people used to sit, behind the house of the Prophet ﷺ. They used to worship day and night. So when the Prophet ﷺ used to go out of his house in the morning, for the early morning prayer, at times he did not look at them. Then God told him, "No, look at them. They are worshippers during the night and workers for Me during the day."

That verse shows us the importance of gnostic knowledge of God—knowing yourself and knowing your Lord. As the hadith says, "whoever knows himself knows the greatness of His Lord."

And that is why the imam just now was reciting the last several verses of the the Chapter of the Cave, Suratu'l-Kahf and he mentioned in the recitation:

> *Say (O Muhammad!): "If the oceans were ink*
> *(wherewith to write out) the Words of my Lord, sooner*
> *would the ocean be exhausted than would the Words of*
> *my Lord, even if We added another ocean like it, for its*
> *aid."*[55]

The Prophet ﷺ knows himself. And knowing himself, he knows the greatness of His Creator. And with that knowledge, even if all the oceans were ink and all the trees were made into

---

[53] Suratu 'l-Kahf (The Cave), 18:28.
[54] Arabic: *Ahlu 's-Suffah*: The People of the Bench.
[55] Suratu 'l-Kahf (The Cave), 18:109.

pens, they would not be enough for him to describe his great knowledge of the greatness of his Lord.

When he saw that greatness, he said, "I am but a human being, [You sent] revelation on me." He wants to tell us a message, "Do not be ignorant by being proud of yourself. I am the Messenger of Allah, the one who ascended by God's Power on the Night Journey and Ascension. He took my body up, against all the physical laws of this world, and caused me to penetrate this atmosphere, going through the whole universe without affecting my body."

Look at the space shuttle that was destroyed because it experienced a little bit more heat than it could withstand. So what kind of shuttle did the Prophet ﷺ have? No plane, no rocket, no shuttle—he had nothing to fly him – only the *buraq*[56]. He went from earth to the heavens and came back.

Yet, with all this, he said, "I am not proud. I am but a human being." He did this to show us how to be humble.

Yes the Prophet ﷺ is a human being, but "revelation came to me." There is a big exception here, for he is different from all of us. He receives revelation from God!

In the hadith of Jabir, when he asked the Prophet ﷺ "what was the first thing that God created," the Prophet ﷺ said:

> The first thing that God created was my light, O Jabir. And from one part of that light, He created the pen, from one part He created the throne, from one part He created

---

[56] The heavenly steed that carried Prophet ﷺ to the heavens on the Night Journey and Ascension.

Paradise and Hell and from one part he created [the rest of creation.] [57]

We are not going to delve into this topic now. Suffice it to understand that he said, "And with all that God gave me, I must still see myself as nothing before Him."

Our problem today is that if we know a little bit, we begin to think we know everything, and we argue and debate. This is the illness in the Community of Prophet ﷺ today, and it makes the community clash within itself—because each person has an opinion.

We can continue longer, but it is a principle that must be only forty minutes, or the hearts of people begin to go here and there.

I was explaining something, today, for a book that is coming soon, and I will end with this: today's physicists say that there was a big explosion in this universe—the Big Bang. According to this theory, there was a big explosion and this entire universe came to be.

Okay. Let us accept it as they say. What is it that exploded?

When you explode something there must first be a substance that explodes. You cannot have an explosion of nothing. Where is the actual element that exploded? So it means there was something there.

And by God's Will He says to a thing, "Be," and it will be.[58] It came out. So there must have been something. We will come back to it later. When that something exploded, God said "*kun*—be!" and then it moved.

---

[57] 'Abdu'r-Razzaq's *Musannaf*.
[58] *See, e.g.*, Surah YaSeen, 36:82.

So when the Big Bang exploded, it moved. And we know this universe is a vacuum, so that means it should have moved forever. If you push something in a vacuum it keeps going. What kind of driving force stopped everything in its place? That is something from God's Greatness.

Think about it; if you put something in a no-gravity zone and push it, it goes forever.

> *Do not the Unbelievers see that the heavens and the earth were joined together (as one unit of creation), before We clove them asunder?*[59]

So when they say there is a Big Bang in a gravity-less and frictionless zone, all of the particles in that explosion should keep moving. But instead the components of the universe are still in their places. What stopped everything at the right time and position? And what was it that exploded?

We come back to the hadith, "The first thing that God created is my light." That is when we reach that reality of excellence in understanding knowledge of God. That is when we begin to see that we are nothing. We are very weak and very small. Whatever you are becoming—doctors or engineers or scholars or *muftis* or imams or presidents or kings, we are still nothing.

That is why the Prophet ﷺ divided religion into three aspects: Islam, Faith andPerfection (moral excellence). If you want the first level of Paradise; you can achieve it by practicing the obligations—the five pillars—of Islam. If you want to go higher, you must add faith to it.

---

[59] Suratu 'l-Anbiya (The Prophets), 21:30.

If you want to reach *maqaʿdi sidqin*—the station of prophets, trustworthy ones, and the witnesses who testify, you have to reach perfection, moral excellence, sincerity.

Our duty is to perfect our belief. If we perfect our belief, everything will open.

Fear God, be pious, and then He will teach you.[60]

That is something great. It means that God will give you knowledge that you never expected to have in your heart.

As God mentioned in a hadith from Him:

My servant draws not near to Me with anything more loved by Me than the religious duties I have enjoined upon him, and My servant continues to draw near to Me with supererogatory works so that I shall love him. When I love him I am his hearing with which he hears, his seeing with which he sees, his hand with which he strikes and his foot with which he walks. Were he to ask [something] of Me, I would surely give it to him, and were he to ask Me for refuge, I would surely grant him it. I do not hesitate about anything as much as I hesitate about seizing the soul of My faithful servant: he hates death and I hate hurting him.[61]

Knowledge will appear on your tongue that no one can speak of.

This is what we are after and this is what we seek. May God grant us that. May He bring all Muslims together—not just physically but spiritually also, and protect us from the turmoil and confusion that is coming in front of us, and save us from any

---

[60] Suratu 'l-Baqara (The Heifer), 2:282.
[61] Bukhari.

kind of difficulty and from anything that is not in our hands; may God take it away from us and keep us safe in our communities and countries.

The Symphony of Remembrance in the Era of Shah Naqshband

Obey Allah, obey the Prophet, and obey those in authority among you.[62]

We hope we will be on the way of obedience. Everyone looks at obedience as if he is obeying. He looks at it without good consideration. Obedience varies from one person to another. For example, here we have two cups of water, and the cups are different. But the water is the same—water is water. The form of the cup changes, but the water is the same.

So what really changes is the outside—the container's shape and capacity.

Similarly, as the Prophet ﷺ said: "Souls are like a group of people together, like gathered troops. Those that recognize each other among them come together, and those that do not, differ."[63]

All of these souls come from the same ocean, the Ocean of Power. One of God's names is *al-Muqtadir*—the Absolutely Powerful, with absolute power in His Hands.

So all of these souls are coming from that ocean, and their origin is the same. All are human spirits. But the difference is how much they achieved during their lives, after God sent them to

---

[62] Suratu 'n-Nisa (Women), 4:59.
[63] Muslim.

this world and these souls entered into a form. This form changes from one individual to another—the form of the body.

Each body is different—how much has God put into your body of selfishness, how much each body was able to play with the soul, and how much each body was able to either make the soul achieve higher levels of sincerity or, in the other direction, to move away from sincerity to heedlessness, and how much is it going to lean towards egoistic and bad desires.

For this reason, when God created Adam ﷺ, He left him in Paradise for as long He wanted, before sending the soul. The angels used to see a form without a soul, without movement. And also Satan used to see Adam ﷺ in that state. When God sent the soul into the body, it made the body move to see how much the body would run after its desires and how much it would be able to keep sincerity—for many, many years until Satan came and whispered in the ear of Sayyidina Adam ﷺ.

> *In the result, they both ate of the tree, and so their nakedness appeared to them: they began to sew together, for their covering, leaves from the Garden:* ***thus did Adam disobey his Lord, and allow himself to be seduced.***[64]

Adam ﷺ disobeyed God by eating from the tree whose fruit God had prohibited him from eating. Breaking that prohibition made Adam ﷺ fall into disobedience. What happened? God cast him out of Paradise, which He made prohibited for him, and sent him to our world—because in Paradise there is no sin.

---

[64] Surah TaHa, 20:121.

That is why when we look at ourselves and hear the voice of God in Holy Qur'an saying *"Obey God, obey the Prophet and those in authority;"*[65]– that is not a simple order.

Adam ﷺ was a prophet and when he disobeyed once God sent him from Paradise to this world. So obeying is not so easy.

Try to progress through your life toward the way of the Prophet ﷺ, following his footsteps and slowly, slowly achieving more. Then, through that achievement, God will bring you near. When God brings you near, He increases the love in your heart for Him and for Prophet ﷺ.

Why do we listen to each other? Because we love each other. Two people listen to each other because they love each other. A student listens to his shaykh because he loves his shaykh. Without love there is no obedience. This does not come for free. You must work for it. People are not working for it and yet they complain "O, we are not improving."

That is because you are not trying to increase your love towards God and his Prophet ﷺ.

Sayyidina Adam ﷺ disobeyed once, but he repented and God forgave him and sent him to this world. Satan disobeyed many times, but he did not repent and then God cursed him.

Disobeying plus repenting equals forgiveness. Disobeying plus not repenting equals getting cursed.

For this, since we are weak and heedless, we are going to fall into mistakes and disobey, but quickly we have to repent because of the formula above, that disobedience plus repentance equals forgiveness.

---

[65] Suratu 'n-Nisa (Women), 4:59.

But if we disobey and stay in that disobedience, and are happy with it, then we are going to cry in the afterlife.

In this world, they leave you to do what you want. You disobey, no problem. Do whatever comes to you, whatever you like. God showed you through His Prophet ﷺ what is permitted, *halal*, and what is prohibited, *haram*.

> *Say (O Muhammad)!: "This is my way: I do invite unto Allah,- on evidence clear as the seeing with one's eyes,- I and whoever follows me.* [66]

But the Prophet ﷺ said, "If you knew what I know, you would laugh little and cry much..."[67]

On Judgment Day when God calls us, everyone will be shaking and worried. If you want to believe, believe. If you do not want to believe, that is up to you. Everyone is worried—is he going to be saved or he is going to be thrown into Hellfire?

If you think your actions in this world will put you in Hellfire in the afterlife, that means you are in a big problem. That is why the Prophet ﷺ said, "If you knew what I know... you would stop enjoying yourself and would go out in the streets praying to God," [68] meaning "you would work only for the afterlife."

How long will you live? Sixty or seventy years; one hundred at the most?

I know someone from our followers—his father was 99 years old. What did he take with him? Nothing. Are you going to live longer than 99 years? Even 100 years becomes like a second.

---

[66] Surah Yusuf (Joseph), 12:108.
[67] Tirmidhi.
[68] *Ibid.*

But eternal life is not like a second. Because 99 ends—that is why it is like a second—but eternal life does not end, that is why it is enduring. It never ends. So what do you want to do?

God said:

> *But teach (your Message) for teaching benefits the Believers.*[69]

That reminder will benefit them and God will straighten their ways and God is the Forgiver. Whenever you ask for forgiveness, God will forgive you. But you do not know if between disobedience and repentance you will pass away. If you die at that crucial moment then you do not know what will happen. You will be lost.

For that reason, saints are always worried for their followers. They want the best for them. They want them to achieve for the afterlife.

That is why the training and discipline of a shaykh varies from one shaykh to another. Each has a different taste and a different way of working with everyone. It is enough to be in the circle of the shaykh, around the shaykh, around the teacher, even if the teacher tells you to go get firewood, it is enough, if that was your assignment to do that, to raise you up through your stations without your feeling it and without your awareness.

It is not for you to question why the shaykh treating one follower one way and another one a different way. And that is why you see that shaykhs have thousands of followers. They build up one in one way and another in a different way.

That is why there are so many traditions. Prophet ﷺ did not relate every hadith to every Companion. He was giving different

---

[69] Suratu 'dh-Dhariyat (The Winnowing Winds), 51:55.

ones to each. He gave one instructions to suit him and his situation while to another Companion he gave something different. It depends on the circumstances of the time and place. That is why there are Companions that did not hear some traditions. And when such traditions began to move around after the Prophet ﷺ passed away, the Companions were surprised.

Now we know the classification and overall picture—after the scholars classified and organized them. Now you have an overall picture which is different from what the Companions had during their time with the Prophet ﷺ.

The Prophet ﷺ treated each one differently. The knowledge that was taught depended on the size of the container that each one had. He prepared them. He put that light into their hearts.

So after the Prophet's ﷺ time no more Companions could appear. The Companions are those who saw the Prophet ﷺ. After them came the 'Followers'[70], who accompanied the Companions during their lives. Then came the 'Followers of the Followers'[71] who accompanied the Followers of the Companions during their lives. By this means, step by step until today, that knowledge was transferred to us.

Now there are saints who became the holders of that knowledge.

Three Weekly Gatherings of Remembrance

Saints give to each follower according to his capacity. They see who is able to carry and who is not and lift them up, increasing their levels through attendance at their circles, their meetings.

---

[70] *At-Tabi'een* in Arabic.
[71] *Tabi' at-Tabi'een* in Arabic.

That is why in the time of Sayyidina Shah Naqshband, he had three sessions a week. In one session they used to come and do *dhikrullah* silently. They had a big center in his mosque—whoever visited Uzbekistan with us saw it—and they take a shower and dress in white clothes afterwards, because any clothing worn while walking in the streets will carry negative energy. The shaykhs prefer you wearing clothes not previously worn and contaminated. So after taking a shower and dressing in fresh clothes they come in, sit and do *dhikr*.

They sit for one or two hours and do their personal daily liturgies. You do not hear any sound—it was as if you were under the ocean. And the shaykh was looking at all his followers and how their hearts were moving with the *dhikr*—like musical instruments—not like the crazy music of today, but like the *daff*[72] or the flute. The shaykh can hear when the disciple's heart is doing the personal daily liturgy, through *dhikrullah*. It is as if you are blowing in the flute or like moving the bow over the violin strings—it yields a melodious sound. These personal daily liturgies, *dhikrullah*, when they pass over the "strings" of the heart they yield beautiful, heavenly tones.

The saint knows that sound, and he knows his followers by the musical tones their hearts make. Music here is a metaphor, not to be taken literally. That is the sweet individual sound of that disciple's soul. Our physical sound, however, is like that of wild animals—when we talk and shout and show hatred for each other.

But the heart sound, no one can hear except those God wants to give to them the ears to hear.

The second meeting was held Monday, Thursday and Friday. That means Sunday evening, Wednesday evening and through

---

[72] *Daff*: flat drum.

the night of Friday. The second meeting was for meditation[73]. During these sessions, the students would not make even the slightest movement. Nothing. They would sit on their knees, hands on their thighs, connecting their hearts with God's love, Prophet's ﷺ love, the shaykh's love, and their friends' love. They would feel that light and the good energy that was circulating in that special room. They would sit one, two or three hours, depending on how much they could take; disconnected from the outside world, unable to hear any sound. Rather they were given special inner hearing by God, by means of their continuous practice and worship.

The third meeting was receiving advice from the shaykh.

In these three meetings Shah Bahauddin Naqshband raised them up. During the day he would make those who were without jobs work—on anything. Giving work is like using a fishing rod—he would throw it out and use it to catch them.

He would pray, "O my Lord, these ones are helping me, help them. These are working for me and helping me for my way and my way is following your Prophet's ﷺ way; help them."

The supplication of the saint is acceptable. Allah says:

Call on Me, I will answer your prayer.[74]

We are sinners, so our prayers are not accepted. But for the saint, Allah says, "I am listening."

So achievements come through such meetings and through the supplications of the shaykh. This takes us to love of God, love of the Prophet ﷺ, love of the shaykh and love of the students. That

---

[73] Arabic: *Muraqabah*.
[74] Surah Ghafir(the Forgiver), 40:60.

brings us to obedience. Otherwise obedience is only through the tongue but will not be reflected in actions.

May God grant us obedience in our actions. May He grant us love for Him, His Prophet ﷺ and His saints.

STOP LAUGHING, BEGIN TO CRY

[Shaykh addressing a gathering in a mosque for remembering the Birthday of the Prophet ﷺ (Mawlid an-Nabi ﷺ)]

Obey God, obey the Prophet, and obey those in authority among you.[75]

God we know, and the Prophet ﷺ we know, but who are "those in authority"? They are the ones who show you the good, show you the bad and show you the correct way.

If someone is showing you the good, then he is in authority. He is telling you not to follow the bad way—the way of Satan. He is telling us, "Follow the way of Allah."

The first of those who are in authority is the father.

The Prophet ﷺ said, "Everyone is a shepherd and each one is responsible for his flock." [76]

That means the head of the house is responsible for his family, his children. Your child looks at you, he does not look at anyone else. Your child is looking at you—you have the authority. If a man does not have authority on his children, then it may be he does not have authority on himself.

---

[75] Suratu 'n-Nisa (Women), 4:59.
[76] Bukhari and Muslim.

Today, parents are not following what the Prophet ﷺ showed us—they are becoming lenient and soft; both on their children and on themselves.

Teach Islam to Your Children

Now you see children do not go to the mosques, do not study Qur'an. For what reason? They do not study knowledge, for what reason? Because the parents are not doing that. They will say, "You are not studying, so why should I?" And we are saying we want to fix the Muslims' problems – and wondering why Muslims are behind.

I was giving the Friday Prayer sermon today, and I mentioned what the Prophet ﷺ did when this verse of Qur'an in the Chapter of the Star was revealed to him. God said *Do you then wonder at this recital? And will you laugh and not weep?*[77]

This verse is as if God is saying, "Are you doubting what We are revealing to the Prophet ﷺ? Is this where you have arrived, O My servants? Are you laughing and doubting the Qur'an?"

That was in the Prophet's ﷺ time—what do you think about today? Today, no one is taking care of the Qur'an. And we want to be successful. How are we going to be successful?

You are wasting your life in entertaining yourself. You are not thinking about the afterlife at all. You only cry when you are afraid or when something tremendous happens.

So what do you think about Judgment Day? Are you not going to cry on Judgment Day? You **are** going to cry there.

But people now are not interested in the afterlife.

---

[77] Suratu 'n-Najm (The Star), 53:59,60.

Now, in this time, you go to mosques. What do they speak about other than politics? Some say something nice, but mostly they are only focusing on politics. Are you going to be able to change anything? You can change nothing.

The Prophet ﷺ said, "If the sultan is bad, **pray** for him to change or to be taken away."

Now, everywhere they are demonstrating in thousands and hundreds of thousands—in Egypt, Indonesia and in many other countries, yet no one is listening.

What you have to do is to increase your zeal or enthusiasm towards the afterlife, because this world is only about laughing (and not crying) and being heedless. You are heedless of what is going to come.

The miseries you are seeing today are not even one percent of what is going to come as related in the predictions of the Prophet ﷺ. Not even one percent. And yet people are not thinking of their afterlife.

Remember Death

And the Prophet ﷺ came out of the mosque one time, as today, when people go out of the mosque, how they stand together and speak. He saw them standing together and laughing. He stopped and said: "Increase remembrance of the Angel of Death." [78]

Increase the remembrance of the Angel of Death and the remembrance of death itself. The Prophet ﷺ was telling the

---

[78] Abu Na'eem relates a similar tradition, where the Prophet said, "Increase your remembrance of the destroyer of delights." We said, "O Prophet of Allah, what is the destroyer of delights?" He replied "Death."

Companions: "Remember death and do not stand about wasting your time."

On another occasion, he ﷺ came out of the mosque and saw people standing and laughing, and he said, "If you knew what I knew, you would laugh little and you would cry a lot..."[79]

That is the Prophet ﷺ speaking. The Prophet ﷺ was laughing little and crying a lot, and now all of us traditional Muslims say that we love the Prophet ﷺ and that the most important thing is the love for Prophet ﷺ; and we attack the Wahhabis because they do not respect and love the Prophet ﷺ.

It is okay, it is good—they say that you have to love the Prophet ﷺ, but let them apply it experientially/experimentally on themselves. Not by nice speeches on love of the Prophet ﷺ, and love of the Family of the Prophet ﷺ, and love of *Mawlid* (the celebration of the month and date of his birth). You must experiment, and be the one to do it; you must be the first to do practice it.

How do you show love of the Prophet ﷺ? By excessive worship. He used to worship until his feet were swollen.

> *O you who have wrapped up in your garments! Rise to pray in the night except a little, Most of the night. Half of it,- or a little less, Or a little more; and recite the Qur'an in slow, measured rhythmic tones.*[80]

"Half the night or less" means to begin by 11 o'clock or 12 o'clock or a little bit less. At least after midnight or 1:00 o'clock.

If we say we love the Prophet ﷺ, then what about the verse:

---

[79] Tirmidhi.
[80] Suratu 'l-Muzzammil (Folded in Garments), 73:1-4.

He who obeys the Messenger, obeys Allah?[81]

The speakers were speaking of love of the Prophet ﷺ. Did they give up all that they have for the Prophet ﷺ? Imams today speak of love of the Prophet ﷺ but where is the reality of this love? It is becoming a profession—that is what I am seeing. It is becoming a profession to speak on love of the Prophet ﷺ, but not to act on it. Not all of them do that; many of them are first in observing their duties.

That is our duty—to raise our children. To raise them in the right way, in the right manner in loving the afterlife more than this world. Or else we will be lost.

I remember when I was young—four years old—I used to pray the late morning prayer—Duha prayer—behind my uncle. We were raised in that manner. Eight cycles of prayer before the noon prayer. My uncle was head of religious affairs in Lebanon and I used to pray behind him. Today if we cannot raise our children like that then we are losing. I am not saying that to converts—rather to those who were raised as Muslims. After all, converts might have come into Islam with their children already grown up.

The problem of the community today is we are not following the reality of what the Prophet ﷺ showed us. We take the shell and leave the fruit. We say we are doing everything from Islam, but no.

When you want to achieve a higher level, you must pass the obligations, to the second level which is faith, and then you must pass to the third level, which is perfection of faith, sincerity. Otherwise we are not able to understand the reality of the message of Islam. Today the community is lost. They are in too

---

[81] Suratu 'n-Nisa (Women), 4:80.

many problems; they are straying too far from religion. But still in this country we see sincere people putting up mosques, teaching their children and advocating for Islam.

May God forgive us all and take away problems from Muslim countries and make it easy on those who are suffering that pain, suffering from fire.

Who is a Martyr?

> The Prophet ﷺ said, "...anyone who dies in a fire is considered a martyr, and anyone who drowns is considered a martyr..."[82],

So fire is a great pain and a great misery. May God make it far from every person. We saw the danger of fire in Lebanon for 17 years. We know what that suffering means. We were living under the constant bombardment of rockets and bombs. We suffered and lived through that.

To those who have not lived in it, I will explain that the experience of it is that it shakes the heart. They have special bombs which make the heart shake. When you hear those bombs, you know that everything is coming down, collapsing. And we were in the basement.

May God protect the Muslims and the non-Muslims. May He make all people to live in peace.

---

[82] Ahmad, Abu Dawud, al-Nasa'ee.

GUIDE YOUR FLOCK TO THE RIGHT WAY

Obey Allah, obey the Prophet, and obey those in authority among you.[83]

Those who are in authority are those who advise you to do what is good and prevent you from doing what is bad. Those who advise you to do good, they show you the way that you have to follow in order to follow the footsteps of Prophet Muhammad ﷺ, in order to reach God's love.

And with every one of us, that authority begins within the house.

The Prophet ﷺ said, "All of you are shepherds, and all of you are responsible for your flocks."[84]

That statement means that all of you have authority on your families, and must show them and direct them to the right and good way. You are responsible, and liable, for this authority that God has entrusted to you. There are only two ways: the way of God and the way of Satan.

God showed what is *halal* and what is *haram*. You cannot say that God did not tell you the difference. If you want to do *halal*, it is obvious; and if you ant to do *haram*, that way is also clear.

The husband is responsible for the wife, and the wife is responsible for her children.

---

[83] Suratu 'n-Nisa (Women), 4:59.
[84] Bukhari and Muslim.

God said:

> <u>Men are the protectors and maintainers of women</u>, because God has given the one more (strength) than the other, and because they support them from their means.[85]

God gave men the authority of protection on the wife and the family—to raise a family, and from a family to build a community, and from a community, a nation.

If we do not follow this way, we will lose. What is the sign of winning and losing in this arena? It is what we are facing today of miseries and problems around the world. There is no safety. The entire world is worried about what will happen next. What will happen, what should they do tomorrow?

Those who are in progressively higher levels of authority, from the husband, the head of the family, to the community, to the city government and onwards, upwards to those in authority over the entire state in every place around the world—if that authority is not good or right, then everyone will fall down.

You must not be like Pharaoh and Nimrod. Pharaoh said, "I am your Lord, most high"—we must not be like that and let our ego to be in authority on us.

> *And proclaimed: "I (Pharaoh) am your lord, most high."*[86]

God did not create anything without wisdom. He created us from a very pure element, and we have to give that pure element back. When the Prophet ﷺ was asked "What did God create first?", he said, "Allah created my Light first."

---

[85] Suratu 'n-Nisa (Women), 4:34.
[86] Suratu 'n-Nazi'at (Those Who Pull Out), 79:24.

The Prophet ﷺ said, "First, God took a handful of His light and created me from that light."[87]

We are showing how pure that element from which humanity is created, and how humanity is trying to darken that element which God wanted us to return to Him clean—as clean as it was when He gave it to us.

People today say, "We must love Prophet ﷺ, we must do *Mawlid* for the Prophet ﷺ," but that love should not come only from the tongue; it should also come from the heart—and we must act on what we are saying.

God put that light into us, and dumped us into the Ocean of Power. And God spoke to the light of Prophet ﷺ, and He left it to turn in the Ocean of Power. In the ocean you have whirlpools. They spin very, very quickly. God left the Prophet ﷺ light to spin with full speed in that ocean of Power.

How can we circumambulate around the Ka'bah? That light was circumambulating around the essence of that attribute, the **attribute** of *qudrah*—not around God's Essence. The name of *qudra*, from *al-Qadir*, the Most Powerful—the absolute power is in God's Hands.

He created everything from that power.

Prophet ﷺ is describing that "God left my light circling in that ocean." Look how pure that is. So when something turns very quickly, what will it accumulate? Energy! It was accumulating, accumulating more and more energy, energy, energy; as it accumulated energy, there was no way except for it to explode. That was the 'Big Bang'. That energy that was accumulated from that light was built up into expansion, and that is what the

---

[87] Mentioned in Ibn Jawzi's *Mawlid al-'Arus*.

Prophet ﷺ said, before creating the pen, before creating anything else, God took that light and created the pen, the throne, angels and heavens, and from one fourth of that power He created creation—from the light of the Prophet ﷺ.

God said in the Holy Qur'an,

> *With power and skill did We construct the Firmament: nd, verily, it is We who are steadily expanding it.*[88]

> *And of every thing We have created pairs: That ye may receive instruction.*[89]

He said, "the heavens, the skies, the firmament, we have created *bi-aydin*—'by hand.'" This means *qudrah*—not by God's Hands. Although God used the literal word "hands," the verse means "with power." Prophet ﷺ said, "He created creation from that light," and God said, "We have constructed the firmament and We are expanding it."

When that explosion happened in that vacuum in which when there is no friction, everything should have moved without ever stopping; instead it continued with full force.

God's order is between the *Kaf* and the *Nun* of "*Kun*" ("Be"). Be and it will be. When God said *Kaf*, that explosion of the light of the Prophet ﷺ took place, after it had been accumulating, by spinning, this energy of *qudrah*. And it shattered, in this vacuum which became the whole universe.

The letter *Kaf* was the driving force of the elements of that explosion. The theory of the 'Big Bang' says something exploded but they do not know what it was that exploded. There must have

---

[88] Suratu 'dh-Dhariyat (The Winnowing Winds), 51:47.
[89] Suratu 'dh-Dhariyat (The Winnowing Winds), 51:49.

been something there to explode, and that was the light of the Prophet ﷺ, condensed into mass.

And the letter *Nun* was the opposing driving force, which opposed the action of the outward motion and stopped it all from moving. And that does not stop the movement completely, because still creation is continuing; there is a driving force still driving particles and there is a force stopping them.

That is the meaning of *Malik al-mulk*, King of the Kingdom, and the Creator is continuously in creation, from that light. Stars stop, planets stop, others continue, it never ends.

Only on Earth can people live, from all of this universe. It is the same as someone with a wild tree, who wants to bring a fruitful branch and graft it on wild the tree. When Sayyidina Adam ؏ came to Earth, there were traces of the soil of Paradise—that beautiful element—so that as soon as his feet touched Earth, Paradise was grafted with the Earth. That is why only the Earth is alive and not the other planets of the solar system—it was grafted with heavenly power.

God wants this trust rendered to Him as He gave it to us. He is sending birds to eat the heads of those who in authority who are not guiding their flocks in the right way.

From the level of the household up to the level of entire nations, from the lowest level to those who are in authority; from those who are not correctly raising their families, to those in charge of nations who are not supervising their charges correctly—against those who do not return that trust as pure as God gave it, God is sending special heavenly elements that will eat their heads. This means a kind of disease that spreads around without people's knowledge—it will affect only those who are on the wrong way. Those on the right track are those leaving the forbidden, *haram*, and doing only what is permitted, *halal*. This refers not only to those above us; but the wife is responsible for her husband and children, and she must tell him if he is not following the right path. Similarly, the other way — she is responsible and he is responsible. If they do not properly carry that responsibility, that bird is going to come and sit on their heads and eat.

From nowhere, worms come from the birds; birds are coming from heavens and spreading all kinds of difficulties for those who are not on the right way.

We must not tell ourselves "later" … and then, "O… we were not aware of it." No. We must correct ourselves. Everyone on earth must correct themselves — time is running short. There is no more time to wait, anymore — it is beyond the hands of people.

This is going to escalate, and suddenly everything is going to come to a head, to a crisis. Many things will fall apart.

Those who are on the right way, God will reward them. Those who are on the wrong way, God will call them and take them away. Only good ones will continue to live on Earth, and there will be peace on Earth for many decades. O people! Do not think that God does not take His revenge. He gives time but He eventually takes His revenge.

> In the time of the Prophet ﷺ, when the unbelievers were attacking the Prophet ﷺ at the Battle of Uhud, they threw stones at him and broke his front teeth. God ordered Sayyidina Gabriel ؏, "O Gabriel, go in the fastest way to prevent the blood of the Prophet ﷺ from falling on the ground. If it falls on the ground there will be no more life on earth, no more vegetation." And Gabriel ؏ said, "that was the quickest I ever went to earth, to catch and hold the blood of the Prophet ﷺ." Otherwise everything would have frozen and died.

That pure blood of the Prophet ﷺ is flowing in the community of Prophet ﷺ, through his children and grandchildren and through his daughters.

Prophet ﷺ used to look at Sayyidina al-Hassan and Sayyidina al-Husayn ؓ and say, "they will be martyrs"

And he said, "These two sons of mine al-Hassan and al-Husayn will be the masters of the youth of Paradise."[90]

They killed them. They made their blood flow on the Earth. They dragged them and cut off their heads. They did not leave one piece of their bodies without cutting it. Especially Sayyidina Husayn ؓ. They let his blood flow in the streets of Karbala.

God told Sayyidina Gabriel ؏, "Stop the blood of the Prophet ﷺ from reaching the earth."

What do you think of the blood Sayyidina Husayn ؓ, it is going for nothing?

God spoke of Habib an-Najjar in the verse,

Then there came running, from the farthest part of the City, a man, saying, "O my people! Obey the apostles;"[91]

His grave is in Antioch, Turkey—you have to go 1,000 steps down to visit him.

God destroyed the whole city, the whole village of those who harmed this Friend of God. What do you thing of someone who harmed Sayyidina Muhammad ﷺ? When you harm his grandchildren, you harm him!

They dragged Sayyidina Husayn ؓ—they dragged him and they dragged others from his family.

---

[90] Ibn 'Asakir.
[91] Surah YaSeen, 36:20.

I am not speaking about politics. But the the land where the grandchildren of the Prophet ﷺ were harmed, and the Lord of the Prophet ﷺ is taking His revenge. He is punishing them, and His punishment is taking whoever is there.

Therefore, that pure element that God gave to us from the pure light of the Prophet ﷺ—we must take care of it. Otherwise, different kinds of diseases and elements and plagues will grow on earth, and disaster will befall.

Those problems are in front of us. Keep with your family and children. Do not interfere in politics. Do not interfere in things outside of your home. Concentrate on raising your children and concentrate on your home.

This year began on a Tuesday—the first of Muharram, 1424. Tuesday is the day of blood, it is well known. And this year is the year of blood; until this illness is removed from the earth. May God show us the good days and take away from us bad days.

Saints are expecting a big opening from the horizon declaring the coming of the Mahdi ؑ. That is not going to take too long. Insha-Allah it is coming in the near future.

And we will be a part of that future peace, God-willing.

RAISE YOUR CHILDREN IN INNOCENCE

[A speech in a new Afghan Mosque in Hayward, California]

And frustration was the lot of every powerful obstinate transgressor.[92]

That is a verse that refers to tyranny.

Praise be to God, when I entered this mosque I was very happy. It has been perhaps nine years since you began planning this mosque and I passed by here and saw the land that you had set aside for it. When I entered it I saw its beauty and those nice decorations and that is something that makes the heart happy.

And the Prophet ﷺ was always asking people to decorate themselves for prayer,

> *O Children of Adam! wear your beautiful apparel at every time and place of prayer.*[93]

God said, *"wear your beautiful apparel,"* and the word He used in Qur'an was " which can mean either "the best of clothes" or "the best of what looks nice."

And you can find such beautiful mosques in New York and Washington, but you cannot find mosques decorated like this in this area.

When you decorate a mosque,

---

[92] Surah Ibrahim (Abraham) 14:15.
[93] Suratu 'l-'Araaf (The Heights), 7:31.

And the places of worship are for God (alone)[94]

When you decorate a mosque, you are decorating for Allah. The Mosque of the Prophet ﷺ, in Madinah, is decorated. And in Mecca, the Honorable Ka'bah is decorated; and the blessed black cloth that covers the Ka'bah is decorated. It is decorated with the nicest cloth and the finest gold, every year. And these represent and symbolize the house of God.

God said, as the Prophet ﷺ mentioned, "Neither My heavens nor My earth contains Me, but the heart of My Believing Servant contains Me."

It means that the heart is a house to be decorated. You cannot pray when your heart is not decorated. If anything dirties your heart, it means the light that God has put there will be extinguished. Tyranny is one of those things.

Tyranny is anything that stops the light that God put in the heart of the believer; it extinguishes and veils that light.

God said,

God is the Light of the heavens and the earth.[95]

"Allah is the Light." It does not mean that God is light, but His Attribute *an-Nur*, the Light, illuminates the heavens and the earth. God's Essence, no one knows. God can be known through His Names and Attributes, nothing else. There is no way to know His Essence however.

The Creator created, and human beings cannot know Him except through His Beautiful Names and Attributes, His Descriptions.

---

[94] Suratu 'l-Jinn (The Jinn), 72:18.
[95] Suratu 'n-Nur (The Light), 24:35.

When God says *"God is the light of heavens and earth"* that light mentioned here is from His Beautiful Names. When He says that He is the *Nur*, light, that means everything in heavens and earth must contain that *Nur*. Are we on earth or not? If we are on earth, then that light is in us.

That light is included in every individual. One of His names is al-'Adil, the Just. He cannot give only to you, and neglect me. God gives to everyone.

And that is why the Prophet ﷺ said, "human beings are born on innocence. His parents make him either a Jew or a Christian or a Zoroastrian."[96]

That means each human being is carrying that light of faith and Islam.

God did not say "...born in innocence **when his parents are Muslim.**" No, He ﷺ said, "His parents make him either a Jew or a Christian or a Zoroastrian." The child is born Muslim. That light is already there. But the problem is that our parents, who are responsible for us, extinguish that light by the manner in which they raise us. And that is how we became tyrants to ourselves. We do not know what is good for ourselves and what is bad, because we have not been raised normally or correctly. Now praise be to God, some people are raising their children in a good way.

But we have many problems in the Muslim community. That light that God put into their hearts has been destroyed. Though that light will never disappear, it is veiled and it has to be brought out once again.

---

[96] Bukhari and Muslim.

Like you are here in the mosque and it is bright, with all these lamps. When we were outside we could not see that light—it is veiled. Similarly, the heart of a human being is full of the light of Islam that God has given to it but from our own tyranny from and over ourselves, we cannot see that light.

That is why the Prophet ﷺ said, "Beware the vision of the believer, because he sees by the light of God."[97]

God gave some people, whom he described in the Holy Qur'an as, "Men who kept their covenant with their Lord:"

> *Among the Believers are men who have been true to their Covenant with God. Of them some have completed their vow (to the extreme), and some (still) wait: but they have never changed (their determination) in the least.*[98]

Where are such people today? Look at anyone today; if he sees something he does not like, he jumps against you—he wants to fight. Or he gets angry. Anger is very bad. When someone gets angry with his family, with his wife or children, he becomes like someone who is drunk. He cannot think anymore. You are fighting now with your anger. At that time your weapon is your anger. Anger is from Satan, it is not from the Merciful[99].

One of God's 99 Holy Names is 'the Patient'.[100] The Absolutely Patient—God is showing that patience to His servants. From Adam ﷺ until today, if you go back in history, how many years

---

[97] Tirmidhi and at-Tabarani.
[98] Suratu 'l-Ahzab (The Confederates), 33:23.
[99] 'The Merciful' (*ar-Rahman*) is one of God's Holy Names. Because it rhymes with Shaytan, the name for Satan in Arabic, the two names are used in the same sentence to juxtapose the choice of being good against dissipation into evil behavior.
[100] *As-Sabbur*, the 99th Name of God.

can you go back? You are educated—how many years? Go through history, trace your way.

They say humans have been on earth for millions of years, but it is not correct. Where are the traces of millions of years? The only ancient civilizations we see are the Phoenicians and that relating to Pharaoh. If there were previous civilizations, where are they? If there was something living before that, where is it now?

Human beings have a beginning and an end. Do not think there is no end. Yes, there is an end. People are making plans for the future, but God said:

> *The Hour (of Judgment) is nigh, and the moon is cleft asunder.*[101]

If God says *"the Hour is nigh,"* then we agree that it is approaching.

No? Who said "no"? From the time of the Prophet ﷺ until today, 1,400 years have passed. Do you believe that the community of Prophet ﷺ can exist much longer? It is already falling apart.

Between Prophet Jesus ⚔ and Prophet Muhammad ﷺ, 600 years elapsed. And before Jesus ⚔, prophets were coming in quick succession, one after another. Yet now, 1,400 years have elapsed since the Last Prophet ﷺ, and he said, "I have been sent close to the Judgment like these two fingers."[102]

No, there is no more time.

---

[101] Suratu 'l Qamar (The Moon), 54:1.
[102] Bukhari.

You have to encourage people for their afterlife, not for this world. The Prophet ﷺ did not come to prepare people for this world, he came for their afterlife.

How much longer do you want to live? Seventy years, eighty years? Then you are dying. So do you want to be dying under tyranny or dying in tranquility?

Dying in a state of tranquility means to follow the footsteps of the Prophet ﷺ. If we are truly following the footsteps of the Prophet ﷺ, we must decorate our hearts, in the same way that this mosque is decorated with *dhikrullah*.

God said:

> *Those who believe, and whose hearts find satisfaction in the remembrance of Allah. for without doubt in the remembrance of Allah do hearts find satisfaction.*[103]

Peacefulness comes from *dhikr*. *Dhikr* can be recitation of Qur'an. Are we doing that? Are we sitting and reading Qur'an daily? No. Perhaps some people are. O Muslims, if we want God to support us, we must do better.

We must not think too much. They took the lead. And we must take the lead. It is not taking the lead to go out and protest. That is not the lead—that is a political situation. If you really want to protest it is best to protest against Satan's influence in your heart.

Rabi'a al-'Adawiyya was one of the famous lady saints of Islam. Her husband died, leaving her a widow, and the scholars of her city came to her. They used to come to learn from her. And they told her, "O Rabi'a. You have to marry." And this is correct, according to Shariah. You cannot be without a husband nor can a

---

[103] Suratu 'r-R'ad (Thunder), 13:28.

husband whose wife died be without a wife. That is the *sunnah* of the Prophet ﷺ.

She said, "I do not have time for marriage." They said, "What do you mean?" She said, "I am busy," and they asked, "with what?" She said, "I am busy in asking forgiveness." They said, "What do you mean by that?" Rabi'a was asking forgiveness 24 hours a day. She said, "My asking for forgiveness itself needs forgiveness."

They told her, "O Rabi'a, you still have to marry." She said, "If you can answer my questions, I will marry."

They said, "What are your questions?"

"These are very basic questions," she replied.

Men, even you are naturally like that. We run more to this world than to the afterlife.

She said, "When God orders the Angel of Death, Azra'eel ؑ, to come and take my soul, will he come with punishment or mercy? If you give me an answer then I know what I have to do."

No one knows.

She said, "Very well. Leave that. If you have no answer to that then, when the Angels of the Grave, Ankar and Nakeer come to me in my grave and want to question me, are they going to come with punishment or with mercy?"

Who knows? No one.

She said, "Okay, leave that question." On Judgment Day, where God said:

> *Then shall anyone who has done an atom's weight of good, see it! And anyone who has done an atom's weight of evil, shall see it.*[104]

Is He going to call me to account with mercy or with punishment?"

So no one could respond to her questions. Do the scholars know? What answer could they give, except to say "you will be called to mercy with the intercession of Prophet ﷺ"? Even they did not know if the Prophet ﷺ would make intercession for a particular person. So they kept silent, and she said, "I am busy asking forgiveness."

That is a simple example to learn. How many times are we asking forgiveness a day? Maybe not at all.

How many sins will we make once we exit this door, when we look left and right? You go shopping, you go to the mall, and you are seeing everything in front of you. Men and women naked, jogging in the streets. Is this a sin or not? Are you remembering to turn your face and say *Astaghfirullah* (Your forgiveness, God)? No, instead you are continuing to look.

Is staring at them accepted, Islamically, or not? So that small example is enough to show whether or not we are living with piety.

A Secluded Life

In Madinah the Enlightened, may God bless and grant peace to the one who is there, there was a fortress, like the old *dhikr* houses. In this fortress were mostly Afghans, and people from Central Asia and Bukhara. That was the fortress where they

---

[104] Suratu 'z-Zalzala (The Earthquake), 99:7-8.

would come to stay during Hajj time or ʿumrah. I used to go there always, because our shaykh always made seclusion there. It was called *Madrasa Ash-Shuna*. Our shaykh made seclusion there for one year, not going out except for prayers. He ate seven olives a day and one piece of bread for one entire year.

Shaykh ʿAbbas Qari lived there for more than 125 years. He was a Mojaddadi-Naqshbandi. When he was 75 or 80 he married an Indian woman. He had one room that people would sit in and visit him, plus his bedroom and a bathroom.

The lady that he married entered that room and never came out except the day she died. For 27 years she never left her room. She was busy in God's remembrance, *dhikrullah,* and recitation of Qur'an.

I know that because I was there, and I knew that man very closely. Where can you find that kind of man or woman today? Because of that, our sincerity is going down. Because of losing that sincerity, the community of the Prophet ﷺ is falling apart.

Very few are still maintaining such sincerity.

Fear God, be pious, and then He will teach you.[105]

There are a few, like for example some old people. When we become old we become afraid of the afterlife. But young people never think like that. If you think of that when you are young, then when you become old you become a saint, because you have kept yourself from falling in the hands of Satan.

"...He will teach you."

When you read Qur'an or hadith, your heart will be inspired with something that you never expected.

---

[105] Suratu 'l-Baqara (The Heifer), 2:282.

O people, not everything is from the outside. The body is vanishing, the soul is living. The Prophet ﷺ said, in a hadith *Qudsi* (the words of God):

> My servant continues to approach Me through voluntary worship until I love him, and when I love him I become the eyes with which he sees, the ears with which he hears, the hands by which he touches.[106]

O Muslims, increase your voluntary worship. You have to do your required actions, whether you like it or not—they are obligatory. If you do **not** do them, you are under a question mark. But your voluntary worship—you do not have to do it, but if you do it then God may give you special rewards.

May God support us; help guide us to the way of Islam.

This life is ending. No one is going to live forever. If you do good, you will find good; if you do the opposite, your afterlife may be in question—and you do not want your afterlife to be in question.

> Sayyidina 'Umar ؓ said, "If your actions of today are not better than yesterday, then better for you to be below ground than above."

> One day Sayyidina 'Umar ؓ come home crying. His wife said, "O 'Umar why are you crying? Today they vowed allegiance to you as leader of the believers."

Nowadays people do not vow allegiance. Leaders compel allegiance to themselves by force. That is why the Muslim world is under tyranny. They glue themselves on their chairs. What—are you happy with that leadership?

Do not approach leadership, it is dangerous.

---

[106] Bukhari.

Sayyidina 'Umar ؓ said, "Today is my heaviest day. If one person in the desert or jungle is sleeping hungry, I am responsible. If someone is dying out of hunger, or from any problem, I am going to be asked first about it. What will I answer?"

So what is today's leadership going to answer when confronted?

Sayyidina 'Umar ؓ did not want that leadership.

How many people today are sleeping hungry? How many are being killed without reason? Thousands are being killed without reason, only because other people want to kill. For what reason? That is how God is going to check the Muslims. For the non-Muslims, never mind—they are under their own burden of their unbelief. Do not bother with it. Forget about them. Their Creator will judge them. Look at yourself. Be busy with yourself and with the community of Prophet ﷺ; are you doing good or not?

That is the problem. Who killed Sayyidina al-Hussayn ؓ, Sayyidina al-Hasan ؓ, Sayyidina ''Uthman ؓ, Sayyidina 'Ali ؓ? They killed the companions and family of the Prophet ﷺ.

Who killed them, the non-Muslims?

May God forgive us. May He keep us in the guidance of Islam—traditional and correct Islam.

Many difficulties are going to come in the very near future. A lot of problems and a lot of killing. And at the end, God and His Prophet ﷺ and Islam will be strong.

> *And say: "Truth has (now) arrived, and Falsehood perished: for Falsehood is (by its nature) bound to perish."*[107]

Haqq is coming—Truth.

Sayyidina 'Umar ؓ said, "Are we on the right way or wrong, O Messenger of God? If we are on the right way, I will make the call to prayer from the rooftops."

Do not think that God's angels are not working for bringing truth. Do not think that will take more than twenty more years. All the signs of the Last Days have appeared—whatever the Prophet ﷺ mentioned, line-by-line. I was compiling these hadith. There are more that 1,000 hadith of the Signs of the Last Days. Some of them are very strong hadith, some are good, some of them are fair, and some weak. But there are around 1,000 hadith.

All of them show what is happening today and what has taken place in the past ten years, until today. From that we must understand that we are coming to an end. There is no more time to trade anymore. When Prophet Jesus ﷺ comes, the time to trade is ended. The time to trade is now. From those hadith, the end comes with the appearance of Prophet Jesus ﷺ. When he appears, everyone is going to be either with him or against him.

So the time of trade is now. God knows our hearts. What we say on our tongues, and what we speak, in different groups of leaders, God knows if it is right, and God knows if they are making conspiracy or not.

Shaykhs; true scholars; sincere scholars, are busy with asking forgiveness, afraid of what is going to happen in the near future. A child's hair will turn white from what is going to happen of

---

[107] Suratu 'l-Isra (The Night Journey), 17:81.

horror and revenge. Those who are going to be protected will be protected—they are under Divine safety.

When God wanted to protect His House, the grandfather of the Prophet ﷺ 'Abd al-Muttalib ؓ said, "O my Lord! That is your house. You are responsible for Your House. I am responsible for my camels. I cannot do more than that; I am weak. You take care of Your House."

What happened? Allah sent down birds upon the encroaching army, carrying rocks in their beaks and in their claws. In the explanation of Imam Suyuti, he said that these were what we call today guided missiles, smart bombs, that were spinning so fast that red color coming out of them, like guided missiles—1400 years ago Islam had that technology.

And the name of the person targeted by each rock was written on it. It will not hit anyone unless his name and his father's name is inscribed there. Do you not think that if God wants to protect us, He will not?

If it is written to protect us, He will do that.

Even if a bomb falls here, He will veil it. When the Prophet ﷺ was ordered to migrate from his hometown, as he left he threw sand in the eyes of the enemies, and recited:

> *And We have put a barrier before them and a barrier behind them, and We have enshrouded them in veils; so that they cannot see.*[108]

Do you think that verse will not protect us? Why will it not protect us, when God sent the Qur'an for that?

This is an ocean.

---

[108] Surah YaSeen, 36:9.

Everything is making praises of God—everything. Now my explanation might be different from that of others, but for me, when God says, *"there is not a thing but celebrates His praise,"*[109] that means everything, living or non-living. And those which we see as non-living are in fact living, because after all they make praise of God. Even the sand, rocks and minerals; the cells in the ocean, are going to make praises for God.

And not only are all things reciting phrases of praise, they are also making circumambulation, *tawaf*. If you look at the electrons in the atom of any element, they are encircling the mass at the center the nucleus. And they are moving counterclockwise, like the circumambulation around the Ka'bah. And that mass at the center is from the Ocean of Power:

> *To God We belong, and to Him is our return.*[110]

Therefore we must be balanced in body and soul. The stations—Islam, Faith, and Sincerity—must all be in perfect balance.

That is why *"there is not a thing but celebrates His praise but you cannot comprehend their praising."* That is because you have not improved yourself to reach that level.

> *And He is with you wheresoever you may be. And God sees well all that you do.*[111]

This verse means you are always under His observation.

---

[109] See: *The seven heavens and the earth, and all beings therein, declare His glory: there is not a thing but celebrates His praise; And yet you understand not how they declare His glory! Verily He is Oft-Forbearing, Most Forgiving!* Suratu 'l-Isra (The Night Journey), 17:44.
[110] Suratu 'l-Baqara (The Heifer), 2:156.
[111] Suratu 'l-Hadid (Iron), 57:4.

In the Hadith of Gabriel[112], at the level of sincerity, we are told to "worship God as if you see Him, and if you do not see Him then know that He sees you." The relevant point from this hadith is that "you are not with Him, but He is with you."

Instead, you are with your ego. That is why you must loosen yourself from your ego to realize He is with you. Before you accomplish this, there is no unity, which is a shameful waste, *haram*. The Creator is not in need of creation, but creation is in need of its Creator.

---

[112] Bukhari.

WHERE IS MOSES?

Obey Allah, obey the Prophet, and obey those in authority among you.[113]

This is a clear message to us as human beings that we have to obey Our Creator.

Artificial things are going to go. Reality is going to stay. You cannot destroy what is ever-living. You cannot destroy something that God wants to exist always. God is bringing this entire universe down. He is not going to leave the firmament that we are seeing as it is. Everything is breaking into pieces. As God said in Qur'an,

When the Sky is cleft asunder![114]

It means that what you are living on today will not be here tomorrow. It is like this cup, [holds up plastic cup] and this big pitcher. Which one do you throw away? The plastic cup. The pitcher that has the water—you do not discard it. It is going to stay, because it is more important than the plastic cup.

So everything is going to go, as God said, from the universe that you are seeing:

When the Sky is cleft asunder; When the Stars are scattered; When the Oceans are suffered to burst forth; And when the Graves are turned upside down;[115]

---

[113] Suratu 'n-Nisa (Women), 4:59.
[114] Suratu 'l-Infitar (The Cleaving), 82:1.

Why are the graves turned upside-down? To restore that plastic cup, that one day was present, for Judgment Day. Everything is gone, and then God brings you back, saying, "Come here."

> *Verily, unto God do we belong and, verily, unto Him we shall return.* [116]

We are going back to where we originated. Our origin is the Ocean of Power. That never goes away—it is always there. It is one of God's Attributes from which God brought creation forth. Whatever you are seeing is coming from that place, the Ocean of Power, from one Divine Attribute.

And God created first the light of Sayyidina Muhammad ﷺ, as Sayyidina Jabir ؓ said in the famous hadith. That light, which God made to turn in that Ocean of Power, was always in continuous circulation, turning. From one fourth of that light God made this worldly creation, as the Prophet ﷺ mentioned in the hadith.

It means we are going back to that ocean. When someone dies, that plastic cup, meaning the body, is thrown away. Where is it thrown? In the grave. That means it is of no importance. What is important is the soul, which God takes.

When that soul comes to the womb of the mother, no one knows. Every child is different. And when it goes, no one knows.

You know when the body is conceived; the mother knows when she has become pregnant; she is informed of that. But she does not know when the soul enters the womb. You know when

---

[115] Suratu 'l-Infitar (The Cleaving), 82:1-4.
[116] This is an important saying in Quran; the original Arabic is *"Inna Lillahi wa inna Ilayhi raji'un."*

someone is dead, you can see it, but you do not know when the soul left. That is in God's Hands.

So if that is the case, why then are we not obedient to God? Where are you going to run?

> *That Day shall a man flee from his own brother, and from his mother and his father;*[117]

On that day where is there to run? It means each one is running, saying "O Allah, take them, take all of them to Hellfire, but do not take me!" There will be no one to take responsibility at that time. You will not want to take responsibility for your son or daughter. You cannot take that of your mother or father. You cannot carry that heavy responsibility—you will want to save yourself.

The only one who can carry that responsibility on that day is Sayyidina Muhammad ﷺ

If God grants that to him he will take that responsibility. Perhaps he might take everyone out of Hellfire if he likes. God might grant him that authority. When God gives, He gives at His level of generosity.

Your giving is a test for your heart sometimes—one foot is in front and one is in back, shaking.

When God gives, He gives completely. When He gives His sincere servant, His Beloved, the permission for intercession, what do you think the Prophet ﷺ will do? Will he leave anyone in difficulty, or hellfire? He mentioned the verse,

> *And soon will your Guardian-Lord give you (that wherewith) you shall be well-pleased.*[118]

---

[117] Surah 'Abasa (He Frowned), 80:34-35.

Do you think the Prophet ﷺ will be well-pleased to have a larger portion of Paradise for himself?

When the Prophet ﷺ was born, his mother felt no pain. And two ladies were present with her, 'Asiya and Maryam the daughter of 'Imran, mother of Jesus Christ ؑ. God sent them to the land of the living from the land of the dead in order to be with her when she delivered the Master of the Universe. When he came out immediately he went into prostration.

When Prophet Jesus ؑ was born, they asked his mother the Virgin Mary ؑ about him, he spoke:

> Then she pointed to him. They exclaimed: "How can we talk to one who [as yet] is a little boy in the cradle?" He said: "I am indeed a servant of God. He has given me revelation and made me a Prophet."[119]

If that is for Prophet Jesus ؑ, and God gave him that, then what about Prophet Muhammad ﷺ?

How do they say "that is so big?" They can understand for Prophet Jesus ؑ but they cannot accept for Sayyidina Muhammad ﷺ, coming out of the womb speaking.

We have scholars who are putting themselves down. Those who are in authority over Muslims today, they do not understand the reality of Islam. They have to stand on the right way but actually they play on the fence—they are two-sided. When *Mawlid* comes, they call it "Biography of the Prophet ﷺ."

Say "*Mawlid*—Birthday!" Why are you afraid? *Mawlid* is *Mawlid*. I am observing *Mawlid* and I am proud of it for the sake of our beloved Prophet. They make conferences and call them

---

[118] Suratu 'd-Duha (Forenoon), 93:5.
[119] Surah Maryam (Virgin Mary), 19:30.

"biography,"[120]—that is hypocrisy. That is not accepted. It would be better to sit at home instead of dealing and representing Muslims. How are they representatives of Islam; perhaps they are representatives of Satan.

If Prophet Jesus ﷺ spoke at birth, cannot Prophet Muhammad ﷺ speak at birth? For him it must be higher, he might even speak before birth. If Prophet Jesus ﷺ can bring someone to life, then Prophet Muhammad ﷺ can make all mankind alive! This is our belief. Or else, how can we say we are Muslims, when we humiliate the Prophet ﷺ? When we humiliate the Prophet ﷺ we humiliate Muslims and Islam. That is why we see problems in our countries. That is why we are down.

That is why they do not like me to speak. They boycott me everywhere because we are defenders of truth! We are not afraid. Even if our sustenance were in their hands, still we are not afraid.

Our sustenance, God gave it to our Prophet ﷺ. His name is Abul Qassim ﷺ, which means he is the one who divides the sustenance for humanity. No one can have that name except Sayyidina Muhammad ﷺ.

So of whom should we be afraid? The devils that are leading these mosques? See how they fall, one by one. Those who sit on the fence, and call their *Mawlid* "*Seerah*." While *seerah* is important, call them "*Mawlid*s!"

If you do *Mawlid* every day, every moment, it is accepted. God made *Mawlid* for him every day, every moment. He sent 'Asiya and Maryam, the purest women to attend that holy birth. And He sent not only human beings, but also Gabriel, Asrafil, Azra'eel, and Mika'eel and the angels of heavens. And yet we are shy to make *Mawlid*, to celebrate the birthday of that one to whom

---

[120] *Seerah*, for biography of the Prophet Jesus ﷺ.

God gave authority, the one from whom all of what you are seeing is only one fourth of his reality and immensely more, besides.

So on Judgment Day all that is going to go. God is going to bring back and expose all that is in the graves, when the graves are going to be turned upside down. Scratching and sifting, like the chicken, exposing everything.

It is said that if you put your hand on earth, whatever comes on your hand contains the remainder of a human being. In the form of that dust you are touching human beings.

Scientists wished to understand when the Prophet ﷺ said, "Everything of the human body will decay except the coccyx and from that bone Allāh will reconstruct the whole body."[121] That coccyx is the smallest part of the end of the vertebrate column, the spine. That small bone will not vanish, it continues living even after death.

How it will be living? So today's scientists, they read that hadith and said they had to prove it.

They went to check, and asked a non-Muslim to do the experiment—since they were Muslim scientists they were not of the same level of technology as Western scientists. So they took the coccyx of many dead people and they put it under very high pressure to crush it completely and crushed it to powder under very high pressure. And it is impossible for anything to be living after that kind of pressure. They then checked the powder and found that it contains living elements.

---

[121] *Sahīh Bukhārī* (6:338).

Where is Moses?

They took these coccyxes from Muslims and non-Muslims and cremated them until they were completely burned to ash. They experimented and found that cells within were still living.

That is why he said,

And when the graves are turned upside down;[122]

The graves will be disturbed in order to bring out the coccyxes of their occupants. How did the Prophet ﷺ know that?

Hudhayfa ؓ reported:

God's Messenger ﷺ stood before us one day, and he did not leave anything unsaid at that very spot which would happen up to the Last Hour.[123]

Sayyidina Abu Bakr ؓ used to recite:

"Where is Prophet Jesus ؑ

Where is Prophet Moses ؑ?

Where is Noah ؑ?

O Siddiq, you are a sinner.

Repent to the Master of all, the Glorious."[124]

Sayyidina Abu Bakr ؓ used to recite this all the time, and cry and cry. That was his continuous recitation. One day he was reciting and he disappeared.

He used to recite, crying and crying and crying. And the Prophet ﷺ was looking for him—not seeing him, and looking for him. And then he went to the Ka'bah and he

---

[122] Suratu 'l-Infitar (The Cleaving), 82:4.
[123] *Sunan Abu Dawud, Sahih Muslim.*
[124] Arabic: "*Ayna Jesus, ayna Musa, ayna Nuh, anta ya Siddiq al-'asi, tub ill al-Mawla al-Jaleel.*"

heard him. He entered the Ka'bah and found him crying there. He said, "O Abu Bakr, why are you crying? God named you the Veracious One, as-Siddiq, and He named you my companion in the cave—why are you crying?"

This is the great *Khalifa* of Sayyidina Muhammad ﷺ.

The Prophet ﷺ said, "You are my friend and my companion in migration to Madinah. God gave you all of that importance, so why are you crying?"

He said, "What you are saying is correct. God called me Siddiq. But if God wants on Judgment Day to send me to Hellfire who can stop that? So I have to keep crying and repenting to Allah."

Then the Prophet ﷺ sat with him and both of them were crying.

God sent Gabriel ؏ to Sayyidina Muhammad ﷺ. He said, "Allah is sending his greetings of peace to both of you and saying, 'enough.' Both of you are in Paradise."

And God gave to ten Companions tidings of Paradise.[125]

Do we have such a thing? Do we have a letter saying we are not going to Hellfire? If we do not have that then why are we trying to cause all kinds of problems, for ourselves and to our community—here and in other countries, and making everything crazy in the mosques? Look to your afterlife. It is better to open these mosques and let people go inside and cry.

This world is ending. God is going to bring our body back with the soul that never disappears, and if we were good in this

---

[125] Abu Bakr, 'Umar, 'Uthman, 'Ali, Talha, Zubayr, 'Abdur-Rahman ibn al-'Awf, Sa'eed ibn Zayd, , Sa'd ibn Abi Waqqas, and 'Ubaydah ibn al-Jarrah ؓ

world and followed the way of God, we are saved. If not, cry. Can anyone laugh now?

If you think you are going to be in Paradise now, then go and entertain yourself. If you think that there is a question mark, then sit in your corner and cry. Do you know why saints cry also? They cry not in repentance only, but they cry out of shyness, for how much people are running away from God's mercy and from how much God is sending His mercy over humanity.

He is enough for us—Sayyidina Muhammad ﷺ. Allah sent him as a mercy to the worlds. May God forgive us. May God guide us to the right way.

YOUNG PEOPLE RAISED IN ISLAM

When you spin something what does it generate? Energy. Like a boiling pot of milk—what happens? It overflows. That is how creation came to appear. That is the secret of the Big Bang. I was explaining it from this hadith:

> O Jabir, the first thing Allah created was the light of your Prophet from His light, and that light remained[126] in the midst of His Power for as long as He wished, and there was not, at that time, a Tablet or a Pen or a Paradise or a Fire or an angel or a heaven or an earth. And when Allāh wished to create creation, he divided that Light into four parts and from the first made the Pen, from the second the Tablet, from the third the Throne, then He divided the fourth into four parts [and from them created everything else].[127]

God distinguished seven different groups of people who will be under His shade on Judgment Day. That is very, very important to know. Those who do not reach that shade will be in a terrible situation. If we have that shade, then we will be under God's Mercy.

The Prophet ﷺ said, "Seven will be shaded by God by His Shade on the Day of Resurrection when there will be no

---

[126] Literally: "turned".
[127] 'Abd al-Razzaq in his *Musannaf*. Bayhaqi with a different wording in *Dala'il al-nubuwwah*.

shade except His shade: a just ruler; **a young man who has been brought up in the worship of Allah**; a man who remembers God in seclusion and his eyes are then flooded with tears; a man whose heart is attached to mosques; two men who love each other for God's Sake; a man who is called by a charming lady of noble birth to commit illegal sexual intercourse with her; and he says, 'I fear Allah,' and a man who gives in charity so secretly that his left hand does not know what his right hand has given."[128]

Say: "O God. Shade us under Your Shade on the Day when there is no shade except Your Shade and nothing abides except Your Face." [129] That is what we say during circumambulation of the Ka'bah.

On that day, we will run away, saying "Myself, myself!" Then there is no wife, no children, no father, no mother, everyone will want to save himself or herself. And God will give shade then to the seven groups listed in the hadith above. If we are not from these seven we must expect something difficult.

God will order the sun to descend over the heads of people, burning them. Those who have shade are safe. And one of these groups are young ones raised in God's obedience.

That is why God said:

> *Obey God, obey the Prophet, and obey those who are in authority over you.*[130]

"*Those in authority*" means your guides and scholars. That is why He said, "*He who obeys the Messenger, obeys Allah?*"[131]

---

[128] Bukhari.
[129] Arabic: *Allahuma adhillana tahta dhilluka yawma la dhillun illa dhilluk wa la baqiyan illa wahajuka.*
[130] Suratu 'n-Nisa (Women), 4:59.

The hadith of shade specifically refers to a youth, or teenager, because when you say someone is a teenager, it means what? That he is rebellious and unfocused. But the hadith uses the word *"shabun,"* meaning that young person is hitting the target— focused and directed.

Nowadays a lot of people say, "Never mind, he is 17, 18, 19. No problem. Let him entertain himself. At 25, 30 he will become OK."

God did not say that. Because 30 is beyond the meaning of the word *"shab"* in the hadith, which refers to the one who is on target. The age referred to in the hadith is 15-18. That is the "youth" referred to in the hadith. If someone in that age keeps himself well, then he or she will be under that shade, as the group referred to in the hadith, "A youth that was raised up or kept in God's obedience."

Where can you find such people? They are very few. That is why I am looking at these young Muslims I see here and I am happy to see that they are on the right way. It means they are under that hadith. That means that they are going to have that shade, because they are protecting or preserving themselves from falling now. How old are you? 18, and going and visiting Mawlana Shaykh, and praying. How old are you? [25, 31] So at that age it is very difficult to find obedient young people today.

Masha-Allah, that age, when you are young, is where it is difficult. God will give them shade. It means they are under God's Mercy.

So those who were not able to protect themselves at that age, what do they have to do? They must keep their head in

---

[131] Suratu 'n-Nisa (Women), 4:80.

prostration forever, asking forgiveness. To remember what they have done. How much have you done before?

That is why it is not easy, when people say that "Oh! this one is a saint!" or "Oh! that one is saint!" Who is a saint? You think sainthood is easy, cheap? If you are not following the *sunnah* of the Prophet ﷺ completely, you will never even smell sainthood. And if you have not been raised in obedience, where will you find sainthood?

Many people make themselves gurus. Is being a guru so easy, so simple? Non-Muslim teachers call themselves gurus. They claim to be gurus in their religion, and it is correct. Because they left everything of this life completely, in accordance with their beliefs. They left everything and dedicated their lives to what they believe in, and they disconnected themselves from this world.

Muslims who follow the Wahhabi ideology first of all reject sainthood—and if they are not rejecting it, as some people hold the correct beliefs, they believe this one is a saint or that one is a saint. You find a doctor, and call him a guru; you find a professor and call him a guru. It is not so easy and so cheap.

Guru means saint. It means that he never tried to give a title to himself. As soon as he wants to be respected, it is finished, that one is not a saint.

The Prophet ﷺ did not ask anything from his community. The Quraysh said they would give him anything he wanted if he would leave off teaching Islam. He never asked them for any title. But his actions gave him what God wanted them to give. God gave him the title, He made him the Seal of Messengers.

So saints do not expect people to respect them. And when it comes to them they do not explain it. They act normal. They do not try to promote themselves. That is what is important—to understand the limit of sainthood. How a saint becomes a saint.

I was explaining to someone that we hook the engine to a train, a locomotive. There is the engine and all the other cars are following, wagons in French. They have only a hook to connect them to the engine. They are empty, without an engine. There is nothing there. But since they hooked themselves, they go with the engine. So the engine is what is important.

So when you empty yourself completely, you will be able to hook yourself to the engine. Do not come with a full wagon. The wagon cannot be too full. There must be only one which is full. The others must be empty.

Do you understand or not? No you did not understand.

There is only space for one, not for two. There is no place for "me" and "you." There is only space for one. There is no place for saints with the Prophet ﷺ, there is only the Prophet ﷺ.

"No One" Is Here

Once I went to visit Grandshaykh, Shaykh Abdullah ق. Usually we would go every night or every other night to visit, pray the night vigil prayers and the early morning prayer.

We would pass by Mawlana Shaykh Nazim's ق home and then go. I passed by and knocked and he said, "who is there"? I said, "Me." He did not open the door. Then I knocked again. "Who is there?" "Me." Then I realized. I knocked again. "Who is there?" **"You."**

Letting me in smiling, Mawlana Shaykh said, "There is no me and you here." Do not have an identity in front of saints. Saints have their limits. They see themselves as empty wagons. That is through their belief. They are empty wagons. But because they are empty they are easy to hook. How can you push heavy full wagons to hook to the engine?

Scholars today are like matchboxes—containing a few matches. When you shake the matchbox it makes a sound. They think their knowledge is going to save them and they want to be known, and their titles mentioned. You have to respect them and kiss their hands.

If you kiss the hands and kiss the feet it does not mean anything to the saint. If you empty yourself, and be nothing, then they load on you. But if you come loaded what do you want to do with your garbage, your waste? You are already loaded! Go empty that garbage. Many of today's scholars think they are carrying a big load of knowledge.

They do not know that load has to be thrown away.

O Allah- Open Your Door!

Like Sayyidina Ahmad al-Badawi, as he was approaching his Lord and praying and praying, "O Allah, open Your door," day and night, day and night.

And one day a very simple old man came to him and said, "O Ahmed! Do you want the key for the Divine Presence?" He said, "Yes." He said, "I have the key and I will give it to you."

Sayyid Ahmad al-Badawi was the Grand Mufti of Egypt, a big scholar. He said, "Who are you, why do I have to take the key from you? You do not even know how to read the Opening, Suratu 'l-. I only take the key from the Keymaker, from God when He opens it for me."

"I came to help, if you do not want help that is up to you."

His knowledge made him behave like Wahhabi people. There were no Wahhabis at that time, but his knowledge made him say, "I will go directly."

He was a big saint. So he kept on asking and asking.

Finally he heard a voice saying, "Do you want the key? It is with that servant—I gave it to him. My sunnah in this world is cause and effect."

God makes a cause in order for something else to happen.

"So My will is for that person to have the key for you. Go to him and take the key. Do not come to Me."

That is why guides are very important. Not everyone who calls himself a shaykh is a shaykh.

He went looking for him. Where is he going to look for that simple person? But he was with full *sunnah*. That one was near him, but veiling himself.

Six months he was running, looking for that person. Suddenly that saint unveiled himself and appeared in front of Sayyidina Ahmad al-Badawi. He said, "I have been looking for you."

"I am here."

He said, "I am looking for the key."

"Which key?"

"The key you offered me."

"No, now it is a different key. When I offered it to you you did not want it. Now I want a price for it."

"I will give you whatever I own, but open the Door for me."

"What? You want to give me from the rubbish of this world? I do not need it—God is providing me."

"What do you want then?"

"I want your knowledge that you have acquired through your ego; I want to destroy it. That knowledge you obtained with arrogance. It is molded with your arrogance and pride, so that you became proud of yourself, like a big peacock, a big balloon. Now I have to pinch that balloon."

Ahmad al-Badawi said, "I am accepting." That was the Grand Mufti of Egypt. That saint looked into his eyes and extracted all his knowledge out. Then Ahmad al-Badawi did not know anything. He did not even know how to write his name any more. Even the children were chasing him, mocking him and pelting him with stones.

He did not say anything, keeping all his feelings between himself and saints.

Then after some months that saint appeared again. Allah said: "Fear God and be pious and He will teach you." That saint looked into Ahmad al-Badawi's eyes and poured vast quantities of spiritual knowledge into his heart and mind through his eyes. Then Ahmad al-Badawi became the greatest authority of and knowledge. And no one could look into his eyes anymore. Anyone who tried would faint due to the power coming through his eyes. For that reason he used to wear a veil, *burqa*, to prevent this from happening.

First seekers have to empty their knowledge. When saints want to prepare someone who has acquired a great deal of knowledge, they take all the knowledge from them. When they became ripe then they want to fill him. First they take away everything that person learned.

That is why some scholars become ignorant. Not ignorant, but empty. When they empty them then they can then load them with heavenly knowledge. That is light, like helium. Although helium is a gas, when you blow it in a balloon, what happens? You will fly. That knowledge makes you fly. That is what we must be seeking, not after titles of some people that have named themselves saints. Sainthood comes from Heaven. If I say, "You are saint, you are a saint, you are a saint," it does not make you a saint. It does not mean anything. If you accept people to say that you are a saint, you are misguiding them. God will punish you. Be careful with whom you connect yourself.

I know that in America there are a lot of people who connect themselves now to different kinds of teachers. We see gay people becoming gurus. I heard of many like that. There are people confused of their own identity, as a man or woman, becoming gurus. I heard of many in San Francisco. And you see Muslims who know nothing "teaching" other people.

I keep quiet in the presence of such ones. Mawlana taught us to respect everyone. Our duty is to respect. Whether he has or does not have knowledge, we must be careful. Because we do not want to be misguided. That is very important.

Sayyidina Bayazid al-Bistami ق, one of the biggest saints of the Naqshbandi, was ordered one time to visit a shoemaker; to sit and visit with him. He saw it in a vision, and as he saw he went there, not knowing why. As soon as he approached he said, "O Bayazid, I was waiting for you."

That is in Bayazid's book. "O Bayazid, I was ordered tonight to teach you." Imam at-Tariqat al-Bistamiyya al-Tayfuriyya. How is a shoemaker going to teach him? But they are saints, so he understands. He said, "O Bayazid, for forty years I have been the Qutb on Earth—Allah dressed me with the station of . There are five Qutbs, and He dressed me with that rank."

Bayazid was as a child before him. That shoemaker was a hidden saint. People thought he was a shoemaker, polishing shoes and fixing them. Not a professor, not a doctor, not an imam. Today they come from prison and they become imams.

He said:

> I sat three hours in the company of that shoemaker and he was teaching me. What I learned in those three hours and what God opened to my heart, if I had studied from the beginning of this world to its end I would not have gotten what he gave me.

It means that when sitting with a saint, it is not just what they teach you when they speak; you might sit with a scholar who teaches more. But if he says "Allah" or he says "come sit here," it may be that is enough, or better than sitting with the scholar for ten years. Why? Because they raise you to their level. Whatever they have achieved over fifty years or sixty years or seventy years of worship, they raise you up to that level. So in heaven's sight you are up in that level, although you may no longer even know how to read anything. Because that saint is the engine for you, and the Prophet ﷺ is the engine for all saints. So when you come, surrendering, empty like an empty wagon, he is able to pull you.

A scholar comes, unable to carry even his own weight, full of himself and with knowledge of letters. Satan had knowledge of letters. Satan knows the Holy Qur'an; he knows the Holy Gospels; he knows the Holy Psalms. But what did it benefit him? Nothing—he was cursed. Anyone who has pride or arrogance is inherits from Satan. Anyone who has humbleness has inherited it from the Prophet ﷺ. May God bless us and bless this meeting.

Be Nothing

What is most important is to be nothing. If you ask for something you will never reach it. Buddhists and Hindus ask to reach nothing. That is why God gives them what they are asking—although their path is incomplete, God is merciful. So since they came against their egos, God gives them this world.

But if you as a Muslim come against your ego, God gives you this world and the afterlife.

> *And He has subjected to you, as from Him, all that is in the heavens and on earth: Behold, in that are Signs indeed for those who reflect.*[132]

So in this life Muslims who come against their egos will reach Heavens **and** Earth if they are fighting their egos as people of other religions are fighting their egos. But we do not do that because we are very arrogant.

God is taking revenge on us, not because He likes vengeance but because He is cleaning us in this world in order to purify and cleanse us for our afterlife.

Are we on the way of truth or on falsehood? We are on the way of truth, are we not? So why are we losing? Because God is giving us a hard time, to straighten us out. He is not giving a hard time to others, because they are already wrong. He gave them this world.

So do not be stupid. Take that lesson that God is sending as a warning. Why does everyone come against us today?

The Prophet ﷺ said, "The nations will come against you as people when eating, invite others to share their dish."

Someone asked: "Will that be because of our small numbers at that time?" He replied: "No, you will be

---

[132] Suratu 'l-Jathiya (The Kneeling), 45:13.

numerous at that time: but you will be like foam that is carried down by a torrent..."[133]

It means, with no value. Why no value? Because we lost our faith in God and Prophet ﷺ, and in saints.

God said, in a holy hadith, "Whoever shows enmity to My saint, *wali*, I declare war on him."[134]

So God is declaring war against Wahhabis today, and because they control Muslims, all Muslims are falling apart. Finished.

Nothing is going to be changed until Mahdi عليه السلام comes. There is no way Muslims are going to come out from that deep ditch they are in except by heavenly support.

I wrote a book containing many of the hadith of the Prophet ﷺ about Mahdi عليه السلام, the Last Days and Jesus عليه السلام. We received an email from an Orthodox Bishop of Russia. We do not know how we received that email.

"The head Archbishop of our church in Russia wants to visit you. You assign the date. And we prefer to come in April, because we found that your tradition and our tradition on the Armageddon, the Messiah and Jesus' return are similar and that our mysticism and the mysticism of Islam are similar."

That is why I am going on the 15th; I am meeting him in Lansing on April 16th. He is flying to America, with his group. I think that is because he read that book.

That is the sign—Jews are looking for Armageddon; Christians are looking for Armageddon. But Mawlana Shaykh Nazim is angry because Muslims are not looking for it, although it is a core

---

[133] *Sunan Abu Dawud*; a similar narration is found in Ahmad's *Musnad*.
[134] Bukhari.

of belief in Islam. Not one Muslim is speaking about it. Jews are preparing themselves and Christians are preparing themselves.

Yet look all over the world; not one imam can speak about this subject. Why are Christians speaking? You see only Christians and Jews speaking about it. But in Islam, no one or very few.

How do you want to plan your afterlife without talking about it? No, they are planning for fifty years, or many years into the future—how many Playboy Clubs they will build, and how many casinos they will set up.

Seven Dates

The Prophet ﷺ would eat only seven dates in the evening. He said, "They are protection against illness and from the evil eye." So some scientists want to find out what is behind that.

There must be a reason for everything he did. See the verse of Qur'an,

It is no less than inspiration sent down to him;[135]

So scientists built a machine to digest the dates in the same manner that a human would, so that they could see what happens.

They found that when when digested the dates produce a blue light, and it forms a kind of compound that goes throughout the body and particularly to the liver and to the places of the body in which poison concentrates.

And they found that blue color goes to the affected portions of the mind of psychologically ill people, or people who have been affected by envy.

There are many traditions of Prophet ﷺ that they are studying now and trying to find the secrets behind them.

How did the Prophet ﷺ know these things?

Prophet Jesus ﷺ, Sayyidina Musa ﷺ, none of the great prophets knew this.

---

[135]Suratu 'n-Najm (The Star), 53:4.

The Importance of Marriage

Obey Allah, obey Prophet, and obey those in authority among you. [136]

We are here today to witness a wedding.

Do not come against the country you are in. Many people came here 300 years ago because in their own countries they had problems. Just as in my personal life I cannot stab someone in the back who helped me and opened his arms to me when I had a problem, I cannot turn against the United States after they opened their doors to us and let us in when we needed them.

Every country and every person is looking to America to solve their problems. So then why are we making problems by bringing the problems of the Middle East, the North East and the South East here?

God is in charge of everything and He is planning. He is the Best of Planners. Do you think that you have authority with your opinion to change anything? No.

I was saying yesterday that I was reading through 1,000 hadith of the Signs of the Last Days. All of them predict what is happening today. The Prophet ﷺ showed that these events would happen. Surrender to God's Will. We are peaceful people.

Back to our shaykh's story. You love Mawlana Shaykh.

---

[136] Suratu 'n-Nisa (Women), 4:59.

These two families are Naqshbandis, and they are going to prevail because they are on truth. The Qadiris are also going to prevail because they also are on truth. And Wahhabis are going to fail. I am criticizing Wahhabis because they stand on falsehood—whether they open their mosques to me or not.

You are Sufi people—good people.

Those who are hiding themselves, who are Sufi, and failing to stand up, are keeping a hypocritical stance. They must stand up, or else they are going to put the whole Muslim community in problems.

So the story is, because most of you are Naqshbandi, Sufi people, or traditional Muslims. We accept *Wahhabis* also as Muslim, but they must open their hearts to traditional Islam.

Let us recite a hadith:

The Hour will not be established until a fire emerges from the land of Hijāz which will light up the necks of the camels in Basra.[137]

We are observing this today.

So we come back to our story.

Marry Immediately

Shah Naqshband, one of the grandshaykhs of the *tariqah*, was sleeping at night and heard a voice: "O Shah Naqshband, quickly get your daughter married." That was one thousand years ago.

He woke up. It was a dream in which he heard a voice. The same voice came again. "O Shah Naqshband. Immediately get your daughter married for tonight she became mature."

---

[137] Muslim and Bukhari.

So he woke up and got out of bed. Usually, traditional Muslims, both men and women, cover their heads.[138] He would wear a hat when he was sleeping—and this is correct. You must wear a cap—not the turban!—when you are sleeping.

With the sudden, instruction to find a husband for his daughter, he was confused whether to put his hat on or not.

Why had that vision come to him? Because he was open-hearted.

The Prophet ﷺ said:

Beware of the vision of the believer, because he sees by God's light.[139]

So he heard that voice, instructing him to find a husband for his daughter. So he was running—where could he find a husband for his daughter at that late hour of the night?

Why did he have to hurry? Because even in that time, you could not trust that no sins would take place between men and women. Islam prohibits relations between men and women outside of marriage, just as do all other religions, beliefs and philosophies.

So he ran to the mosque, at 12:00 o'clock, while everyone was sleeping. One person was there. A young man like Zayd here. But there was one difference. That one was poor, and this one is rich.

---

[138] Covering is not only for women. When we go driving in the streets, I see people in London – the woman is covered from top to bottom and the man is dressed in fine Western clothes, and the woman is pushing the stroller. No, the man has to wear decent Muslim clothes and the women also have to wear Muslim clothes.

[139] Tirmidhi and at-Tabarani.

There was only that one person, a young man reading the Holy Qur'an by the light of a candle. He came to that young boy, 18 years of age, and shook him while he was reading. The young man was completely engrossed and was unaware of who had come. He was completely involved in understanding the Holy Qur'an. He kept reading and reading. Shah Naqshband shook him again. He called him, "O Alauddin." He did not respond, for he was diving deeply into the secrets of the Holy Qur'an.

He shook him again, and the young man said, "O my master what is happening?" He said, "Come to my house." He said, "I give my life for you! What is the matter?"

He took him to the house. He said, "O Alauddin, tonight you marry my daughter." Of course he would marry her. He had been worried, thinking maybe this was a test.

He said, "Of course, but I do not have any money for the dowry." He said this because the dowry, *mahr*, is important in Islam—it is a rule that the man must give a dowry to the wife to complete the marriage. Shah Naqshband gave him one gold coin to give to his daughter.

Sayyidina Shah Naqshband ق called his daughter and asked her, "I want you to marry this boy, Alauddin, do you accept?"

The acceptance of the daughter is so important, as we will see from the story of Sayyidina 'Ali's ؓ marriage to Sayyidina Fatima ؓ, later. So that student said to Shah Naqshband when asked to marry his daughter, "Yes, I accept whatever you say."

Sayyidina Shah Naqshband ق said, "I will make the marriage tomorrow." And he made the marriage with two witnesses, the next day. As soon as they accepted, he gave them a medallion of spirituality. God opened their hearts, and alone together, they stayed up discussing the practices of asceticism until they reached the time of the early morning prayer. They prayed the early morning prayer and then they spent their day in asceticism.

Acceptance and Dowry in Islam—
the Example of Sayyidina 'Ali ؓ and Sayyida Fatima ؓ

It is important to ask the girl if she wants to marry or not. Sayyidina Muhammad ﷺ asked his daughter Fatima ؓ whether she was interested in marrying Sayyidina 'Ali ؓ. "'Ali is proposing marriage."

She said, "You are asking me?" He said, "Yes." Because we cannot force our girls to marry people they do not like. Not like some people say today that, "In Islam women have no choice."

Our host listens to his wife. I listen to my wife. I listen to her doubly because she is my shaykh's daughter! [Addressing the groom] Do you listen to your fiancée? Yes. You cannot say that on the first day; you must say, "No, she has to listen to me!"

So the Prophet ﷺ said, "'Ali is proposing to you."

She said, "Are you asking me?"

He said, "Yes, definitely."

She said, "Then I do not accept."

Who can say that, except the daughter of the Prophet ﷺ?

Gabriel ؑ came and said to the Prophet ﷺ, "Ask her why not." Prophet ﷺ asked her. She said, "It is not an issue of whether I want to marry him, but I have conditions. If they are fulfilled then I will marry him."

Look at how this story shows that the children of the Prophet ﷺ carry their blessed father's compassion and love. He said, "what are the conditions?" She said, "O my father, when you were born you were saying, 'my nation, my nation.' When you were ordered to declare your prophecy, you were saying, 'My nation my nation.' And I know when you die you will be saying, 'My nation, my nation.' And I know that on the Day of Judgment you will be saying, 'My nation, my nation.'"

"I want to be part of that expression of mercy to your nation. My dowry for 'Ali ؓ is that the entire community of the Prophet ﷺ will enter Paradise when I enter Paradise."

How can the Prophet ﷺ say "yes"? He had to wait for Gabriel ؏, for revelation. Gabriel ؏ came and said, "O Messenger of Allah, all the community of Prophet ﷺ is in the dowry of Sayyidina 'Ali ؓ."

That is the nature of Islam—to seek the good for everyone, not the bad.

My Advice in Your Marriage

Today my advice to myself and my children is that the life of this world is short. It is going to last sixty, seventy, or eighty years. Enjoy it on the principles that God has made. You (the wife) must treat him well. The wife should look at her husband, and the husband should look at his wife. He should look at the benefit from her, and she should look at the benefit from him.

When the wife and husband are patient with each other, and support each other, you will have such a happy marriage.

Look at this family, Karam and his family, they are raised in a very beautiful environment of Islam. And Munira and her family, are sincere and have a very nice environment. And all of you are getting married. And I will be very happy when I see Aliyah getting engaged and married, following the footsteps of her brothers.

May God forgive us all. And I apologize if I have irritated anyone or made anyone upset, but this message was for everyone—everyone must know that Islam is a peaceful religion.

Are You Building an Ark Like Noah?

It is completely impossible to protect any person against God's revenge. When He wants to take his revenge, He will take it with **force**.

God gives people time—they can come back to the right way. When they do not come back, they are going to find a situation that they do not like.

When you face a problem you do not like it. But you have to remember that before you ended in that situation, God gave you an opportunity to escape. Instead you may say, "Why did this happen." Instead, think about the opportunity that God gave you to correct yourself. Your opportunity now is slipping away.

The Prophet Noah ﷺ said to his son, "O my son, come with us and ride on the ark."

> *And it sailed with them amid waves like mountains, and Noah cried unto his son and he was standing aloof: O my son! Come ride with us, and be not with the disbelievers.*

> *The son replied: "I will betake myself to some mountain: it will save me from the water." Noah said: "This day nothing can save, from the command of Allah, any but those on whom He hath mercy!" And the waves came*

> *between them, and the son was among those overwhelmed in the Flood.*[140]

When the flood comes, who can be protected?

That means that when God's revenge comes, who is going to be protected? When a plague comes, who is going to be protected? Before that plague ends, many people are going to die.

When Prophet Noah ﷺ was building the ark, people were coming to him and laughing.

"What are you building?"

"I am building an ark."

"Building an ark for what?"

"For safety."

"Safety from what? You are building an ark on a mountain!? There is no water there! If you want to build an ark you have to build it by the seashore. You are building it up high on a mountain?"

Then they accused him of having no mind.

That example is a lesson for us (especially for engineers). [laughter] This person here is an engineer—he knows mathematics.

This passage is related to probability. A flood has a very low chance of reaching the top of a mountain. There is an area of science called probability. Do you now probability?

It is the study of the chances of something happening. Only geniuses are accepted into that area of study. Probability is a very

---

[140] Surah Hud, 11:42-43.

highly advanced intellectual logic. Not everyone knows it. In computer programs, all is based on logic.

There are things that have odds of occurring like one in five, one in 10, one in a million. That means that if that experiment is repeated one million times, it can be expected to happen once.

Higher numbers than we ordinarily come across in daily life—after billions, trillions, quadrillions—are expressed with exponents. For example, 10 to the power of 2 ($10^2 = 10*10=100$) would be a 1 with two zeros, or 100. 10 to the sixth power is one million. 10 to the power of 20 (10^{20}) is a 1 with 20 zeros—numbers as large as this go beyond the numbers that we have names for. For this reason we use exponents to express them.

By contrast, 1 over 10^{20} is a number so infinitesimally small that we also do not have a name for it.

The probability of water rising to a height where mountains, animals and people vanish from the earth and become extinct, might be a chance of one over 10 to the power of a trillion ($1 \div 10^{1,000,000,000,000}$). This number equals 1 over the product of 10 multiplied by itself a trillion times, or 1 over the number expressed by a one with a trillion zeros.

Another example of a thing happening that had an incredibly small likelihood of happening is that dinosaurs became extinct. If they lived for millions of years, how did they suddenly become extinct? Where are they now? Suddenly they are gone?!

There are no more dinosaurs, they are finished. There must have been an extremely small probability of the age of dinosaurs ending, and yet it did end. It is gone, they are no longer alive. It means that nothing will live forever. That is the point, the conclusion, of this discussion.

However long human beings will live, there will come a time that what happened to dinosaurs will also happen to us. There is death. There is Judgment Day.

If secular people or non-secular people, Muslim scholars or non-scholars, are not preparing for the afterlife, but only preparing for this world, there is a chance that when Judgment Day occurs, they will be questioned.

The probability exists for everything that it will become extinct. Just as dinosaurs became extinct, so too will human beings on Judgment Day.

As in the Holy Qur'an, the Prophet ﷺ explained the principles of probability via the story of Prophet Noah ؑ. That is the power of Qur'an. There is a very advanced explanation of science in the Holy Qur'an.

They came to Prophet Noah ؑ and asked him what he was doing. "Building an ark," he said.

Are you building an ark? [yes]

Today, all these people, whether secular or not, Muslim or not—is there a probability, or a possibility, that water will come on the mountaintop or not? Yes, there is. Therefore they have to know that there is a probability that they will be brought to judgment, and possibly even thrown in hellfire.

Noah's son is the son of a prophet and yet he says, "No."

For us, the Prophet ﷺ is saying to us, "I will make intercession for you to enter Paradise." We say "No, we do not need you, we are safe with our actions."

Then, based on our own actions, we will go walking, not riding.

A blind man came to the Prophet ﷺ asking him to pray for his sight to be restored. The Prophet ﷺ told him to make a supplication based on intercession through himself ﷺ.[141] "Recite this supplication after you have made ablution and prayed two cycles." The supplication was:

> O Allah, I am asking you and turning to You by means of Your Prophet Muhammad, the Prophet of mercy. O Muhammad, I am turning with you to my Lord regarding my present need so that He will fulfill my need; O Allah, allow him to intercede (with You) for me."[142]

By saying this, the blind man was seeking the intercession of the Prophet ﷺ. This is not polytheism—you are not worshipping the Prophet ﷺ. You are asking God **for the sake of the Prophet** ﷺ—we are not saying that Prophet ﷺ is God's partner.

The above example of Noah and his son is an example. "Come on the ark." He said, "**No,** I will save myself.".

The Prophet ﷺ said, "Come on the Ark of Muhammad ﷺ." The Wahhabis say, "No, we will go by ourselves."

Okay, now let us see how clever they are, the self-appointed scholars, gynecologists, surgeons and engineers, and those who pretend to be the leaders of the Muslims. They are leaders for themselves, leaders of the boat that will take them to the wrong destination. We do not want to go to that wrong destination. We want to go on the Ark of the Prophet ﷺ.

Is that not right?

---

[141] Bukhari.
[142] Arabic: *Allahuma innee as'aluka wa atawajjahu ilayka bi nabiyyika Muhammad, nabiyyu 'r-rahmah. Ya Muhammad inneei atawajjahu bika ila rabbee fee hajatee haadhihi li tuqda lee. Allahumma shaffi'hu fiyya.*

> *And a Sign for them is that We bore their race (through the Flood) in the loaded Ark;*[143]

God is saying, "I have carried them on that sailing boat. That sailing boat is Muhammad ﷺ. If not for him, the whole world; universe is not existing."

That is why when he was asked what was created first, he replied, "O Jabir. The first thing that God created was the light of your prophet."

---

[143] Surah YaSeen, 36:41.

MUSLIMS OF THE WEST ARE THE EXAMPLES FOR THE MUSLIMS OF THE EAST

The Prophet ﷺ used to pray constantly and at length. In one cycle of prayer, he would recite 200 verses of Qur'an. Sometimes he would delay the night prayer and pray long sunnah prayers. He would pray between the night prayer and the early morning prayer, and in between he would pray 8 cycles of prayer and those 8 cycles of prayer would fill that time.

Today we are not doing even one percent of this *sunnah*. Nothing. We are very busy in our lives. Today, as time passes, our children are forgetting the *sunnah* completely, because there are no more scholars teaching its importance. They teach only the five obligations. The scholars themselves are not remembering the *sunnah* of the Prophet ﷺ. We are losing.all of these traditions.

So if we think about how much we have to improve ourselves, like we see today—the main concern of people today is who is going to be sitting on the chair and running the affair of the country. Nothing else. There is no more doing things for God. Everything we do is for politics. Such-and-such politician or such-and-such other politician… Islam became a tool or instrument in the hands of leaders that they use to maintain political chairs.

Islam and religion have become tools in the hands of people which they use to reach their political agendas—nothing else.

And in politics it is well known that you have to lie. What do they call them? "White lies." There are no white lies. There are only three lies which the Prophet ﷺ permitted. First, when you are reconciling between a husband and wife. You can say one thing to the husband and another to the wife, in order to reconcile them. Second, if you are facing danger of attack, you can lie in order to protect yourself. Third, to make peace between two groups that are fighting.

But political lies are not white lies—they are dangerous lies. Politicians try to take advantage of religion and of the trust that people give them.

So let us go back and consider our religion in the light of the importance of this month. This is the month of the Prophet ﷺ, *Rabi' ul-Awwal*. The importance of this month is to remember the life of Sayyidina Muhammad ﷺ and the things that he did in his life for the benefit of the whole community. The Prophet ﷺ did not breathe one breath without it being for the benefit of the community. That is why God referred to him as, *bil mu'mineena ra'ufun raheem—to the believers is he most kind and merciful*.[144]

And those two names, ra'uf, kind and raheem, merciful, are among the names of God Himself. God adorned His Prophet ﷺ from these Attributes, with the aura of those Divine Names. The Prophet ﷺ was *ra'uf*, kind to everyone, soft with everyone. That is why he never closed the door to non-Muslims. He never said, "I am going to fight you." No. He was trying to guide them to Islam.

Drought

The last thing I will say is that when there is a drought, what do you need to cure it—for the earth to have life again? You need

---

[144] Suratu 't-Tawbah (Repentance), 9:128.

water. So the rain is known as the mercy of God, in order to give life back to this dry earth.

Without water, nothing can live. Is that not correct Dr. Nazeer? So when water comes, leaves on the trees bloom, returning to life. And if we think a little bit, we will see that, Glory be to God, the Prophet ﷺ was born in what season? During Rabi' ul-Awwal. *Rabi'* in Arabic means spring.

What comes before spring? Winter. Snow, ice, cold. So winter comes, but then with rain, everything is restored—trees, flowers, plants, forests all spring back to life. Before, in winter, they were dead.

So the rain is mercy. And what is Allah's Mercy? Sayyidina Muhammad ﷺ, who came in the month that means "spring." So Muhammad ﷺ came as a mercy, for giving back life to the whole Ummah, after a drought of ignorance, and after a time of being completely lost, metaphorically in a jungle.

Before the time of the Prophet ﷺ, there was nothing acceptable. Everything was lost, humanity was lost, women's rights were lost, men's rights were lost. It was the life of the jungle, the survival of the fittest. That was life in the time before Islam. The Prophet ﷺ came like a merciful rain, giving light to humanity—and that light will continue to Judgment Day.

That light is there, but no one is looking at it. And so today we are beginning a new era of ignorance. There is no longer that light of Islam, human rights, women's rights, from Islam. Now it is lost. Can you see it anymore? We are in a drought, now. Religion is in a drought. Only the old people go to the mosques. Where are the young?

The young people are in demonstrations, running in the streets, engaged in politics and seeking power. That is where they sent them. They rebel—against anything, no limit to their rebellion. That is a sign of the Last Days.

That is why the Prophet ﷺ mentioned during his life that during the Last Days, ignorance would become widespread. If you have a little Islamic education, people are happy with that today—if you studied a little bit of Qur'an. Where are the Islamic schools that existed before? Now everyone is running after secular science. We are not saying, "Do not study secular sciences," no. But you must study religion with strong effort.

We are saying where are the traditional Muslims, and traditional Islamic practices, like writing poetry for the Prophet ﷺ, and so on? We are no longer following those practices today. Today Islam has become a profession. The real love, burning love, is no more. You cannot find that love any more in people's hearts, nor the fruits of that love. You cannot find that anymore, it is impossible.

People want to build mosques, so they do fundraisers, for which people might give 10 dollars, or 20 dollars. We are not in a bazaar, where they sell vegetables and you bargain. There is no longer love in the way of God.

And the Prophet ﷺ said that there would be too much ignorance in the Last Days. Do we have ignorance or not? Anywhere you turn your face, there is ignorance. There is no more real, basic studies of Islam.

The Prophet ﷺ never instigated hate towards anyone. Today we are full of hatred in our hearts for each other. For what?

Politicians we understand, because they are afraid for their positions. But normal Muslims like us—why do we have to have hatred? We should all be in the same boat.

May God give us the intercession of the Prophet ﷺ.

Without that intercession, it is very difficult to win Paradise. Do not think that by our actions we can deserve to win Paradise. The mercy was given by God to the Prophet ﷺ:

> Adam ﷺ and everyone other than Adam will be under my flag on the Day of Rising.[145]

Why then are we running from the presence of the Prophet ﷺ today?

That means Adam ﷺ and everyone other than him—all humanity. Why are we trying to eliminate the intercession from the Prophet ﷺ. And Prophet ﷺ said, "My intercession is for the big sinners of my community."

O you who submit to God! On the one side we must be very happy, because we are the first community to enter Paradise, by the intercession of the Prophet ﷺ. And on the other hand we must be sad that we are not trying to do better, in order to achieve Prophet's ﷺ good pleasure with us and our Creator's good pleasure with us.

May God forgive us and bless our meeting more and more, and make the lovers of the Prophet ﷺ continue to increase in number.

Look. Today you have Central Asia, near your country Afghanistan. Before they had a communist regime, but now praise to God, Islam is moving back in. And slowly, slowly they are penetrating into these countries. And what is penetrating more is traditional Islam. Because the tradition of Central Asia is classical Islam, traditional Islam. And they inherited that tradition from their parents, which they kept for one hundred years secretly, during communism, and now they cannot accept any

---

[145] *Musnad* Ahmad.

ideology that is coming from a different view, especially the Wahhabi extremist Islam that is being exported from some Arab countries.

Now, unfortunately, some different ideologies are beginning to infiltrate into the countries of traditional Islam. And I will not hide from you, but there are delegations coming to you from these countries, coming to see how Muslims live in America, free to say whatever they wish to say. And they come here, and mostly they are interested to visit traditional Muslims. They do not want to hear the extreme views of people. And that is why in your mosque the delegation of Kyrgyzstan came here, and they are interested to document that traditional Muslims are strong, to learn how Muslims live here and to see how the Muslims here enjoy what they have of freedom.

We have to say that clearly, we cannot hide.

We see that kind of opening for Islam in America. They do not go to Arab countries to see Islam there. They come here, as if Islam is coming from the West. They want to learn from the Muslims of the West. As it is mentioned in the hadith, "The sun will rise from the West." And that is why they are coming, with the sponsorship of the U.S. Department of State, many delegations, coming and meeting with us. They go from mosque to mosque to learn about Muslim life.

What is that influence of Muslim life in the United States on Muslims from Central Asia? They like to see young people, old people, converts all integrating, "no one is better except by piety and good action." Look at all the races in this mosque! That is the beauty of Islam. May God forgive us.

HEAVENLY TECHNOLOGY: SOURCE OF EARTHLY TECHNOLOGY

We are waiting—waiting for a heavenly opening that will come soon, God willing. Soon there will be great changes in this world. For that reason, saints do not let us say anything. They say, "Keep quiet."

The Prophet taught us two phrases that are light on the tongue but heavy in the balance are *"Subhanallah wa bi Hamdihi, Subhanallah al-'Adheem Astaghfirullah."* "Glorified be God and for Him is the Praise, Glorified be the Great, God forgive us."

God informed us that,

> *Taught man that which he knew not.*[146]

This verse is in the first revealed chapter of the Holy Qur'an, which begins with,

> *Proclaim! (or read!) in the name of your Lord and Cherisher, Who created.* [147]

What does the human being "know not"? It means anything that is veiled from him is what he doesn't known. Anything that he knows is not veiled.[148]

100 or 150 years ago, people did not know about airplanes, there was no such thing. Anyone coming up with that idea would

---

[146] Suratu 'l-'Alaq (The Clot), 96:5.
[147] Suratu 'l-'Alaq, (The Clot), 96:1-2.
[148] Suratu 'l-'Alaq (The Clot), 96:1.

have been called a heretic. Anyone speaking about rockets, would have been called a heretic. 60 years ago, people did not know about satellites—people speaking about such things also would have been called heretics.

Anything you do not know about was taught by Him. He taught mankind "what he knew not." It means anything must be known. So everything you do not know, where is that everything?

If forty years ago you had spoken of computers people would not have understood. I remember the first computer at my university. It was the first one in Lebanon, at the American University. It was so huge that it filled a room—it used punch-cards. Really it was an elephant, a huge elephant with less capacity than the ant of today—today's laptop knows more than that huge computer.

Do not assume that you can see all of a person's being. There might be someone who is nothing in the eyes of people, who knows everything. Like that huge computer, bigger than this mosque—that I saw when I was 18 years old. And they put cards into it, which would go through the system. And when they want to do a program again, they would put the cards through the entire computer again. Storing the cards took more space than the computer itself!

And now not only are there more powerful laptops, but even Palm Pilots which have internal recorders, cameras, and cell-phones.

Why do we see that that small Palm Pilot in front of us can do something so huge, yet the huge computer could not?

Why is it that today we cannot accept a saint, unknown to people, and we are running after those who are known, like elephants, like balloons sitting on chairs. They are nothing. They are retarded.

Like these old computers – not one of those old computers is used anymore!

He taught humanity "what they know not." They know nothing. So it means, He taught each person according to his level, according to what he can take. Normal people can take normal knowledge. Scientific people can drink in science. Engineering people can take in engineering. Coffee people can take in coffee. Tea people can take in tea.

And hidden people may take in hidden knowledge.

> *So they found one of Our servants, on whom We had bestowed Mercy from Ourselves and whom We had taught knowledge from Our own Presence.*[149]

He gave him from heavenly knowledge. Why do we have to say "no"?

When you have self-realization, he can manifest in himself all these attributes that God bestows on him for teaching him "what he know not." But first you need that self-realization. You first have to know what is the capacity of your chip.

Do you have a very condensed chip, that can take 20 gigabytes? A chip so small but that can carry millions of items of information? So self-realization can make you condense, to polish yourself, in what the Prophet ﷺ referred to in saying "Whoever knows himself knows his Lord."

Whoever realizes for himself his position of being negative or positive, and understands how to control that egoistic challenging rebellious animal that is inside him—if he can control this then he

---

[149] Suratu 'l-Kahf (The Cave), 18:65.

can begin to destroy it also, and that chip that God has planted in his heart can begin to blossom and to get that information from heavens.

Heavenly Receivers

Metaphorically, that chip has a receiver, a satellite dish. Nowadays, people speaking of computers talk about how much memory you have in your computer. How much memory do we have in the computers in our hearts and brains? What is the evidence that we have such memory and capacity in our brains and hearts? How much information, in gigabytes, do we have? From childhood to adulthood to old age, how much information is stored? Every instant your eyes are open and seeing something, how many pictures did your eyes take in, live, into your eyes?

When you look at something you are recording 30 pictures per second.

If you are 70 years old, multiply 365 times 24 hours times 60 minutes times 60 seconds times 30 glimpses per second (66,225,600,000 images)—that is the minimum that person has seen. Perhaps you see more than that. But also there is your hearing—how many wavelengths did you hear. Everything you heard—every word, voice, and deed, is recorded. Every time you felt something that feeling was recorded.

Every hair you have is a receiver, receiving different wavelengths like an antenna. That is why saints leave their beards—the beard is the receiver of the heavenly power that is coming from heavens. That is why it is advised for men to keep the receivers of positive energy. It is the opposite for women— hair on the head receives positive energy, and they do not want hair on the face. Men have hair on face, as *sunnah*, to receive.

If two women die at the same age and same status, but one has longer hair, respect in Shariah says to bury the one with long hair first.

So these receivers and your eyes are recording; the evidence that they record is stored on you as if you were a chip, and the volume of information that is stored in you could be measured in gigabytes.

> *Then shall anyone who has done an atom's weight of good, see it!*[150]

This means that every atom, every smallest realization or action of a person through the community, what he has seen or heard or sensed, all of his actions and spoken words—all of that is recorded. All that is recorded, good or bad. Not like pictures, at 30 frames per second. No. Possibly one million frames per second are recorded by angels, from the good and the bad that you have done.

So self-understanding, to know what God put us in, and to realize the good and the bad, and to implement what God wants from us through understanding ourselves, by controlling our bad desires and by keeping ourselves from following them, and only allowing our bodies to follow good desires, will end up in lifting the very heavy veils that have filled up and covered over the vision of your heart, sense and sight.

This discipline will throw away those veils, and you will begin to know the meaning of the verse previously referred to,

> *Taught man that which he knew not.*[151]

---

[150] Suratu 'z-Zalzala (The Earthquake), 99:7.
[151] Suratu 'l-ʿAlaq (The Clot), 96:5.

Seeing with God's Light

That is why the saints are like stars on dark nights—they see with God's power, as referred to in the hadith, "Beware of the vision of the believer, for he sees by God's light."[152] When you are in a dark tunnel, you need a flashlight. God is giving you a heavenly light that is referred to in the above hadith, through your power as a believer. The believer sees through heavenly light that can illuminate everything in front of him. Some can illuminate 10 feet in front of them, some can illuminate 100 feet. Some can zoom in or out. Then they have huge spotlights for night-time. And there are more possibilities higher than that, for all of those things are human inventions, which are only weak reflections of the higher realities to which the saints have access.

God said in the above hadith, "… for he sees by God's light." What is that light? A flashlight, a spotlight? It must be sunlight. It is must be even more powerful than the sun—it is God's light. When God's light supports you and follows you, you come to know everything that God wants you to know.

> *So they found one of Our servants, on whom We had bestowed Mercy from Ourselves and whom We had taught knowledge from Our own Presence.*[153]

God gave him from heavenly knowledge, when the servant polished himself.

What comes after "gigabytes" to express more power? Terabytes, danobytes? This shows God's greatness. "Dan." What kind of information do they have of lights and bytes?

So all these different wavelengths are recorded, through all the physical senses that God gave you, seeing, hearing, touching,

---

[152] Tirmidhi and at-Tabarani.
[153] Suratu 'l-Kahf (The Cave), 18:65.

tasting, sensing—it is all recorded. How do they bring this knowledge back after it was recorded?

They press one button, and all of this information pours out in front of you on Judgment Day.

It is not like a computer. No. You will see a real image, what you were doing physically will appear in front of you, as if it was your twin doing it—you are doing it and you are exposed—that wrong thing that you were doing.

May God protect us. That is where the intercession of Prophet ﷺ comes in, to veil us from that bad situation. If you were doing good, that vision will be like a theater; it will not be a theater, no. But everyone will be seeing everything, and saying, "O look at that saint!"

So God hides your wrongdoing. That intercession is for those who have permission. May God forgive us and protect us.

DO NOT DELAY MARRIAGE AND MAKE IT DIFFICULT!

O ye who believe! Obey Allah, and obey the Messenger, and those charged with authority among you.[154]

God orders His servants to obey Him and to obey His Prophet Sayyidina Muhammad ﷺ. Obeying God and His Prophet ﷺ is an obligation—not a *sunnah*—you have to obey. If you disobey, then you are committing a sin, and you will be punished.

And Sayyidina Muhammad ﷺ said many times that the one who is able to marry must not delay his marriage and the one who is afraid that it is too much responsibility which he cannot carry, must be patient; if he cannot be patient, he has to fast.

That is Sayyidina Muhammad's ﷺ message for every time—from his time until Judgment Day. He is seeing that people cannot control themselves. Even in the previous time, people could not control themselves, and that was before all of today's corrupting influences like television, especially MTV, and discos and night clubs, and all these women that are not covered; and all the men who do not care about any morality—in such a time how is it possible for good people to control themselves? So, it is important to listen to what Prophet ﷺ said, and marry.

Today, unfortunately, parents are happy with their children and send them to study in university, which is OK. But the big

---

[154] Suratu 'n-Nisa (Women), 4:59.

mistake is that the boys cannot control themselves. The girls also cannot control themselves, and they become boyfriend and girlfriend, which is not accepted in Islam.

Those who can, even if they are studying in university, can marry. Praise be to God—let them marry young, what is the problem? The parents usually say, "No, they have to wait, until the girl becomes 21, or 22, or 23 and finishes her study; the boy has to wait, and finish his studies." So what are they going to do? Of course, the boys and girls are going to jump over each other.

And adultery is increasing, ignorance is increasing, punishment is coming more on Muslims, because they are not listening to God and the Prophet ﷺ.

God said in the Holy Qur'an,

> *And marry such of you as are solitary and the pious of your slaves.*[155]

The Basis for Tranquility

Marry those who are good from your people around you, both sides, husbands and wives. It is God's order. He said:

> *And among His Signs is this, that He created for you mates from among yourselves, that ye may dwell in tranquility with them, and He has put love and mercy between your (hearts): verily in that are Signs for those who reflect.*[156]

This means, the wife can relax with the husband, so that both will not go out and make sins—this benefit is for her and for him.

---

[155] Suratu 'n-Nur (The Light), 24:32.
[156] Surah Rum (Rome), 30:21.

This way you can be together both in a pleasant situation that God likes and His Prophet ﷺ likes.

God said in the above verse, *"from among His Signs..."* meaning from the signs in His creation of His Greatness, He created "from among yourselves," **from yourself, from your soul, from your body**, "wives" (using the plural form). This means that He gave you, He created for you, wives from yourself. No one can take someone else's wife, if it is not written. God created Sayyidah Hawwa—Eve, the wife of Sayyidina Adam. He created her so that Sayyidina Adam could *"dwell in tranquility with"* or go and relax with her, to see that "this is your home".

She is your home. It means that when you go home, you can relax, you can sit anywhere you like, there is nothing unlawful of whatsoever you do in your home. It is a private place. Your wife is a home for you, protecting you from what is not allowed, protecting you from being cheated and deceived outside. God describes her as a place, a home, where you can go and have your own privacy.

If someone has no home, we say he is poor. If someone has a home, we say that he is rich. God said in Holy Qur'an, "I am giving you a wife from you to be a home for you." This means, "Look after marriage immediately, quickly, when you become mature; your parents must help you look, because they do not want you to be poor. They want you to be rich. By marriage, God makes you rich in His Presence.

When you come and say *"Allahu Akbar"*[157], while praying, and you are married, your *'amal*, good deeds are doubled, because Prophet ﷺ said that marriage is half of the religion, "*Az zawaaju*

---

[157] God is Great.

nisfu d-din—to marry is to complete half of one's religion" which means the married person's religion is doubled.

This way, when you say *"Allahu Akbar"*, and come to prayer, you can do so with no bad desires. *Alhamdulillah*, you and your wife feel tranquil. Both of you have spoken to each other in a way that you can relax and then come to prayer. If you had no wife, you would come to prayer with all kinds of different bad thoughts. "How beautiful is the girl that I work with in the bank!" "How beautiful is the girl I work with in the office!", "How beautiful is my neighbor! I would like to marry her, cheating on my wife." "How beautiful is this one," "How beautiful is that one."

For this, Sayyidina Muhammad ﷺ said, "Marriage is my sunnah (tradition)." It is the way of Prophet ﷺ. "Whoever does not like to marry, he is not following my Sunnah." This also applies to the person who is delaying his marriage, saying, "I am still young, I have to find life, I have to go and waste my time in night clubs and discos. I have to entertain myself, I am so young, I am still 25, I am still 26, I am still 27, I am still 30." He is not following the way of Sayyidina Muhammad ﷺ. As a Muslim, you have to follow!

Flowing Provisions

When you marry, do not worry that provision will not come to you. God will send. God will send provision.

> *Right graciously did her Lord accept her: He made her grow in purity and beauty: To the care of Zakariya was she assigned.* **Every time that he entered (Her) chamber to see her, He found her supplied with sustenance**. *He said: "O Mary! Whence (comes) this to*

you?" She said: "From Allah. for God Provides sustenance to whom He pleases without measure."[158]

God said to you, whenever Sayyidina Zakariyya ﷺ entered the prayer alcove of Sayyidah Maryam ﷺ, he found provision there. When you are keeping the way of traditional Islam, the way of the Prophet ﷺ, God sends provision to you.

> *"I created the jinn and humankind only that they might worship Me I seek no livelihood from them, nor do I ask that they should feed Me. Lo! Allah! He it is that giveth livelihood, the Lord of unbreakable might"*[159].

When you marry, it is worship, because when you touch your wife and your wife touches you, God removes sins. It becomes like taking a shower. It takes all the dirtiness from you, just as your smell goes away by showering. Also, building a family, building a house are worship. Whenever the husband and wife come together, God takes their sins away and writes their time together as good deeds.

God will provide you. You are worshiping Him through marriage, because it is half of religion—you are completing your religion. Therefore do not worry, God will provide you with provision. Do not worry that a child will come, even if ten children come, God sends every child with his own provision.

When you are decent and following the *sunnah* of Prophet ﷺ, God sends from unseen places people who help you in order to receive your provision.

---

[158] Surat Aali-'Imraan (The Family of 'Imraan), 3:37.
[159] Suratu 'dh-Dhariyat (The Winnowing Winds), 51:56-58.

Don't Demand a Big Dowry

Unfortunately today, parents are becoming so stubborn—they do not want to get their daughter and their sons to marry quickly, because both sides put too many conditions on the marriage. They let their children go and commit adultery or fornication outside, behind their backs, because they heap too many conditions on the girl and the boy.

If you go to most of the Muslim world, which should be the best examplar in this world, it is becoming the most difficult place—you cannot marry anymore. The parents demand an apartment, a house, gold, they ask money for their pockets. They ask for a car, they ask for…what? From where can you get all these things?

The boy cannot provide these things, and nor can the girl. Then the parents say, [mimicking an old man's voice] "OK, we can not let you to marry our daughter. We have the girl, if you give us money, you can buy her." Marriage is not something you buy and sell.

"How much dowry are you going to give?"

"I do not know, I have 100 dollars to give, 1 million rupis."

"No! what 100 dollars, (we want) 1 billion rupis, 1 trillion rupis!"

"I do not have it!"

"No—you have to give, or else you can not get our daughter."

From where is he going to get this money? Even to bring a hundred thousand rupis [around 10 dollars] he might not have that in his pocket either.

They put so many conditions, that today boys say, "O, we can never get married." And it is very difficult to commit—how is he going to provide enough for them to get married. Both sides cannot approach marriage any more—it is not only one side.

The parents say, "Look at my neighbor. He is paying 1 million rupies. My neighbor got for his daughter 10 million rupies! So, I have to get at least as much as my neighbor. Either that or I have to be better than my neighbor."

"My neighbor gave a car. Therefore, you also have to give a car."

"I do not have a car, I have a donkey."

"No donkey, it must be a car!"

[Audience laughs]

Is it not true?

So, it is becoming very difficult. The Prophet ﷺ prohibited that.

The Importance of Dowry

If two people agree to marry each other, let them marry. Whatever dowry he can provide, he provides. He can provide whatever he can provide, and cannot give more. If the girl accepts him, and he accepts the girl, it is OK. Finished. The parents must not put problems and obstacles in the way of their children. Do not put problems and obstacles in their way.

There are people who give for the dowry one gold coin for the the pre-marriage dowry and one for the post-marriage dowry. Some people they say one date before and ten dates for after, some people say one silver coin for the dowry. Do not make it difficult.

One of the conditions of the contract of marriage is that you have to state how much you are giving for dowry. There is the pre-marriage dowrhy and post-marrige dowry. Both should be declared. You have to state them to fufill the Islamic conditions of the marriage. So, when people do not have much, they say, "One silver coin before and one silver coin after." It is OK, not causing difficulty for the couple.

And praise be to God, today, we are witnessing the marriage of two people here. One on my right, the other on my left. And I hope they are very happy, and they are completing their religion. And I hope that the husbands are doing their best for their wives, to provide them and keep them decent and honored and bringing, God willing, children who can live in happiness, and become good Muslims.

[Amin]

This is a private arrangement in this house. An Islamic pre-marriage. The official marriage will be made later, by the one who has the authority and permission from the religious ministry. But, I am only doing this as an unofficial marriage in an Islamic way to bring these two people, God willing, together. God willing.

[The ceremony begins- the clock sounded that it was 12 o'clock] Marriage is recommended before the early afternoon prayers, and we ended just at the beginning of early afternoon prayers.

Glossary

'Abd (pl. *'Ibaad*) — lit. slave, servant of the Lord.

Abu Bakr as-Siddiq ﷺ — one the closest Companions to the Prophet ﷺ, his father-in-law, who shared the Hijrah with him. After the Prophet's death, he was elected as the first caliph (successor) to the Prophet ﷺ. He is known as one of the most saintly of the Prophet's Companions.

Abu Yazid/Bayazid Bistami — A great ninth century *wali* and master in the Naqshbandi Golden Chain.

Adab — good manners, proper etiquette.

'Ali ibn Abi Talib ﷺ — the cousin of the Prophet ﷺ, married to his daughter Fatimah and fourth caliph of the Prophet ﷺ.

Alhamdulillah — Praise God.

Allah — proper name for God in Arabic.

Allahu Akbar — God is Greater.

Amir (pl., *umara*) — chief, leader, head of a nation or people.

'Arafat — a plain near Mecca where pilgrims gather for the principal rite of Hajj.

'Arif — knower, gnostic; in the present context, one who has reached spiritual knowledge of his Lord.

Ar-Raheem — the Mercy-Giving, Merciful, Munificent, one of Allah's ninety-nine Holy Names

Ar-Rahman — the Most Merciful, Compassionate, Beneficent, the most often repeated of Allah's Holy Names.

Astaghfirullah — lit. "I seek Allah's forgiveness."

Awliyaullah, Awliya (sing., *wali*) — the "friends" of Allah, Muslim saints.

Ayah/Ayat (pl. Ayaat) — a verse of the Holy Qur'an.

Bayt al-Maqdis — the Sacred Mosque in Jerusalem, built at the site where Solomon's Temple was later erected.

Baya' — pledge; in the context of this book, the pledge of initiation of a disciple (*murid*) to a shaykh.

Dajjal—the False Messiah (Antichrist) whom the Prophet ﷺ foretold as coming at the end-time of this world, who will deceive mankind with pretensions of being divine.

Dhikr—literally, "remembrance" (of Allah) through repetition of His Holy Names or various phrases of glorification.

Du'a—supplication.

Dunya—worldly life.

'Eid—festival; the two major festivals of Islam are 'Eid al-Fitr, marking the completion of Ramadan, and 'Eid al-Adha, the Festival of Sacrifice during the time of Hajj.

Fard—obligatory worship.

Fatihah—Suratu 'l-Fatihah; the opening surah of the Qur'an.

Ghawth—lit. "Helper"; the highest ranking saint the in hierarchy of saints.

Ghusl—full shower/bath obligated by a state of ritual impurity prior to worship.

Grandshaykh—generally, a *wali* of great stature. In this text, where spelled with a capital G, "Grandshaykh" refers to Mawlana 'Abd Allah ad-Daghestani, Mawlana Shaykh Nazim's shaykh, to whom he was closely attached for forty years up to the time of Grandshaykh's death in 1973.

Hadith (pl., ahadith)—reports of the Prophet's ﷺ sayings, contained in the collections of early hadith scholars.

Hadith Qudsee—God's Words relayed on the tongue of the Prophet ﷺ, but which are not part of the Qur'an.

Hajj—the sacred pilgrimage of Islam obligatory on every mature Muslim once in his/her life.

Halaal—permitted, lawful according to the Islamic Shari'ah.

Haqq—truth, reality.

Haraam—forbidden, unlawful.

Haasha—God forbid!

Haqq—truth, reality.

Hijrah—emigration.

Imam—religious leader; specifically, the leader of a congregational prayer. Also an advanced scholar followed by a large community.

Imaan—faith, belief.

Ihsaan—perfected character.

Iraadatullah—the Will of God.

Glossary

Jinn — an invisible order of beings created by Allah from fire.

Jumu'ah — Friday congregational prayer, held in a large mosque.

Ka'bah — the first House of God, located in Mecca, Saudi Arabia to which pilgrimage is made and which is faced in the five daily prayers.

Kalaamullah al-Qadeem — lit. Allah's Ancient Words, viz. the Holy Qur'an.

La ilaha illa-Llah, Muhammadun rasul-Allah — there is no deity except Allah, Muhammad is the Messenger of Allah.

Mahr — dowry given by the groom to the bride.

Maqaam — spiritual level of attainment, station.

Mawlana — lit. "our master" or "our patron," referring to an esteemed person.

Meezaan — the Scale which weighs the actions of human beings on Judgment Day.

Mi'raaj — the Prophet's ascension to the Heavens and the Divine Presence.

Mu'min — a believer.

Murid — disciple, student, follower.

Murshid — spiritual guide, *pir*.

Nafs — lower self, ego.

Nur — light.

Qiblah — direction, specifically, the direction faced by Muslims during prayer and other worship towards the Sacred House in Mecca.

Qiyamah — (the Day of) Resurrection or Judgment.

Ramadan — the ninth month of the Islamic lunar calendar, the month of fasting.

Rasulullah — the Prophet of God, Muhammad ﷺ.

Rawhaaniyya — spirituality, spiritual essence of something.

Ruh — spirit. Ar-Ruh is the name of a great angel.

Sahabah (sing., sahabi) — the Companions of the Prophet, the first Muslims.

Sajda (pl. *sujud*) — prostration.

Salaat — prayer, one of the five obligatory pillars of Islam. Also to invoke blessing on the Prophet ﷺ.

Salawaat (sing. *salaat*) — invoking blessings and peace upon the Prophet ﷺ.

Sawm — fasting.

Sayyid — leader; also, a descendant of Prophet Muhammad ﷺ.

Sayyidina — our chief, master.

Shahadah—the Islamic testification of faith, "*Ash-shadu an la ilaha illa-Llah wa ashhadu anna Muhammadan rasulullah*—I bear witness that there is no deity except Allah and I bear witness that Muhammad is His Prophet."

Shah Naqshband—Grandshaykh Muhammad Bahauddin Shah-Naqshband, a great eighth century *wali*, the founder of the Naqshbandi *Tariqah*.

Shari'at/Shari'ah—the Divine Law of Islam, based on the Qur'an and the Sunnah of the Prophet.

Shaykh—lit. "old man," a religious guide, teacher; master of spiritual discipline.

Shirk—polythism, ascribing divinity or divine attributes to anything other than God.

Sohbet (Arabic, *suhbah*)—the assembly (Association) or discourse of a shaykh.

Subhanallah—glory be to God.

Sultan/sultana—ruler, monarch.

Sultan al-Awliya—lit., "the king of the *awliya*,"; the highest-ranking saint.

Sunnah—the practice of the Prophet ﷺ; that is, what he did, said, recommended or approved of in his Companions.

Surah—a chapter of the Holy Qur'an

Takbir—the pronouncement of "*Allahu Akbar*—God is Greater."

Taraweeh—the special nightly prayers of Ramadan.

Tariqat/tariqah—literally, way, road or path. An Islamic order or path of discipline and devotion under a guide or shaykh; Islamic Sufism.

Tasbeeh—recitation glorifying or praising God.

'Ubudiyyah—state of worshipfulness.

'Ulama (sing. *'Alim*)—scholars.

Tawaaf—the rite of circumambulating the Ka'bah while glorifying God during Hajj and 'Umrah.

Ummah—faith community, nation.

'Umar ibn al-Khattab ؓ—an eminent Companion of the Prophet ﷺ and second caliph of Islam.

'Umrah—the minor pilgrimage to Mecca, which can be performed at any time of the year.

'Uthman ibn 'Affan ؓ—an eminent Companion of the Prophet ﷺ and his son-in-law, who became third caliph of Islam. His rule was renowned for his compilation of the Qur'an.

Wali (pl. *awliya/awliyaullah*)—saint; "friend" of God.

Wudu—the minor ablution that precedes prayers and other acts of worship.

Zakat/zakah—the obligatgory charity of Islam, one of its five "pillars" or acts of worship.

Zakat al-Fitr—the obligatory charity of 'Eid al-Fitr, the festival marking the completion of Ramadan.